EARLY BRITISH SWIMMING, 55

UNIVERSITY LIBRARY DUNDEE

Date of Issue

Early British Swimming
55 BC – AD 1719

With the First Swimming Treatise in English, 1595

By

NICHOLAS ORME

Reader in History,
University of Exeter

UNIVERSITY OF EXETER 1983

University of Exeter, 1983

ISBN 0 85989 134 8

© Nicholas Orme, 1983

The text of Christopher Middleton's *A Short Introduction for to Learn to Swim* is reprinted by kind permission of the Beinecke Library, University of Yale, and the Bodleian Library, Oxford, and the illustrations (from Everard Digby's *De Arte Natandi*) by that of the British Library, London.

Printed and Bound by Short Run Press Ltd., Exeter, Devon

Aeglae, Naiadum Pulcherrimae

CONTENTS

Preface   ix

                                    I

1. From the Romans to the Vikings   1
2. The Middle Ages, 1066-1500   22
3. The Sixteenth Century   46
4. Everard Digby and his 'Art of Swimming'   69
5. Digby's Successors and the Seventeenth Century   92

                                    II

A *Short Introduction for to Learn to Swim*, translated
by Christopher Middleton from Digby's *De Arte Natandi*   111

Bibliography   209
Index   211

PREFACE

An historian who learns to swim in later life must be excused for taking a more historical view of his pleasure than other people. With championship records far beyond his reach, his records have to be the documents about the skill in early times, where alone he possesses some starting advantage. On being taught to swim a few years back, I was moved to wonder how men used to do so and who first wrote a treatise on the subject. The earliest scientific writer was an Englishman, Everard Digby in 1587, a pioneer almost forgotten today, who merits more attention than he gets. The core of this book is an account of his life and work, and an edition of the first English abridgement of his Latin treatise in 1595. From this base I have ventured out to survey the history of swimming in Britain both before and after the sixteenth century. The book begins with the coming of the Romans to the island in 55 BC: the first recorded swimmers in its history. It goes on to discuss their expertise and that of the Anglo-Saxons, the Vikings, the middle ages and the sixteenth century. This is followed by the account of Digby and his work, and the final chapter traces the history of swimming and Digby's influence upon it down to the early eighteenth century. The book is principally concerned with Britain, but references have been made to other parts of the world whenever this seems necessary for the understanding of swimming in the island.

It is hoped that the result will be of use to scholars in several fields. Primarily, it is a record of one of man's major physical activities. Hitherto, histories of sport and physical education, even those that are otherwise good, have rarely had much to say about the period mainly covered by this book: from the end of the Roman empire to the eighteenth century. This reflects the wide diffusion of the evidence for physical skills in that era among sources historical, educational, graphic, literary and religious, often accessible only in Latin, Old French or Old and Middle English. Perhaps one value of the present book will be to draw attention to these sources and to what they yield. Their harvest is by no means inconsiderable. In the case of swimming

there are records from all the civilisations of Britain, from the
Romans onwards, about kinds of people who swam, the conditions in which
they did so, the motives and goals which inspired them, the status of
their skill, and the attitudes of other people towards it. The techniques of swimming are alone obscure, until they too are brought to
light by Digby's book in 1587. What has been gathered here about swimming can easily be matched for other physical exercises: riding, tournaments, hunting, archery, ball-games, athletics and gymnastics. When
such research is done, the history of man's physical achievements will
become much better understood.

The sources are not so plentiful, however, that the historian can
pick and choose what he uses. He has to consult the entire range of
early records to find material for his work, and those which turn up
are casual ones in the context of other matters. These difficulties
are, however, salutary. They make it impossible to write the history
of early swimming as a self-contained topic without relating it to the
societies in which it was practised. In the following pages it will be
seen that there is something characteristically Roman, Anglo-Saxon,
medieval, Renaissance and seventeenth-century about swimming in each of
these periods. Social history throws light upon swimming, and in turn
the history of swimming, once constructed, illuminates the societies
which have practised it. Most of the evidence for early swimming,
moreover, comes from literary sources, including poetry and imaginative
fiction. This obliges the historian to consider not only how swimming
was practised but what people thought about it: in other words the history of ideas. The writers of classical Rome, of early epic and saga,
of medieval romances, Elizabethan drama and the early novel all have
something to say about swimming, and in return the historian can bring
his detailed knowledge of the skill to elucidate their works. For
these reasons it is to be wished that books like the present one may be
found useful by social historians, historians of ideas and literary
critics, as well as by those concerned with sport and education.

This book would not have been conceived without the skilful and
inspiring tuition of Mr B.D. Woods, my colleague and instructor, who
has taught so many people in Exeter to swim or to swim better, thereby
prompting me to take up this research. I am also grateful to Dr M.

Swanton, Mr H.W. Stubbs and Professor T.P. Wiseman for their advice
about classical and Anglo-Saxon sources; to Dr J.J.G. Alexander for
illumination about manuscripts; and to Mr N.C. Buck, sub-librarian of
St John's College, Cambridge, Mr A.D. Hill, senior archivist of Huntingdon County Record Office, and Mrs Dorothy Owen, archivist of Cambridge University, for their helpfulness in forwarding my researches
on Digby. The University of Exeter has once more been most generous
in making it possible for me to publish a book, and it is a pleasure
to acknowledge again the kind assistance I have had from Mr R.A. Ers-
kine, Deputy Registrar, Mrs Barbara Mennell, Publications Officer, and
Professor I.A. Roots, Professor of History. My wife has been my un-
failing confidant and helper throughout.

Nicholas Orme
Brampford Speke,
August 1982

Chapter One

FROM THE ROMANS TO THE VIKINGS

THE ROMANS

There have probably been swimmers in Britain ever since there have
been people. Swimming is such a widespread human skill, and practised by so many societies, that it is hard to believe that the
prehistoric races of Britain did not include a quota of swimmers,
from the Old Stone Age to the Iron Age. The recorded history of
swimming in Britain, however, begins like recorded history itself
with the coming of the Romans. The expeditions of Julius Caesar
and his legions to Britain in 55 and 54 BC brought to the island
its first attested swimmers. The two chief surviving biographies
of Caesar, by Plutarch and Suetonius, were written at the end of
the first century AD, about 150 years after Caesar's death, but
both agree in describing his skill as a swimmer.[1] Suetonius, re-
counting the rapidity of Caesar's movements on campaign, relates
how he and his troops 'crossed rivers which barred his paths by
swimming, or on inflated skins'.[2] Both authors record the famous
incident of Caesar's personal heroism in the water at the battle
of Alexandria, in the winter of 48-47 BC. Forced to withdraw
from a bridge by the Egyptians, Caesar plunged into the sea and
swam to the safety of a nearby ship. 'It is said', relates Plutarch, 'that he was holding many papers in his hand and would not
let them go, though missiles were flying at him and he was impri-
soned in the sea, but he held them above the water with one hand
and swam with the other.'[3] Suetonius, in a similar account,
estimated the distance of the swim at 200 paces (nearly 300 met-
res) and added that Caesar also dragged his cloak behind him with
his teeth, 'lest the enemy should get it as a trophy'.[4] Late as
they are, these stories appear to be based on a credible tradition of Caesar's unusual strength and courage as a swimmer. For

a man in his early fifties, as he was at the battle of Alexandria,
his feat was notable even by Roman standards, which laid a strong
emphasis on the ability of warriors to swim.

Caesar does not allude to any incident of swimming in his own
account of his British expeditions. Plutarch, however, does. He
describes an episode in which the Romans fought the Britons in Caesar's presence beside a marsh or river. The Roman centurions, hamp-
ered by the terrain, were being hard pressed by the enemy when a
Roman soldier dashed into the fight, routed the Britons with many
daring deeds and rescued the centurions. He then returned behind his
comrades with some difficulty, plunged into muddy waters and regained
his own side 'partly swimming and partly wading'. When Caesar and
his men came up to meet him and congratulate him, the soldier fell at
Caesar's feet, begging for pardon; he had lost his shield in the
thick of the fighting.[5] This is the first recorded episode of swimming in British history, albeit from a very late source. For the
Roman conquest of Britain proper, beginning in AD 43, we have the
more contemporary and reliable testimony of Tacitus that swimming
featured in the campaigns. Tacitus informs us that by AD 69 the
Romans were making use of auxiliary troops in Britain contributed by
the Batavi, a Germanic people who lived by the mouth of the Rhine.[6]
The Batavi were noted for swimming with their horses (it is not
clear whether they swam on the animals' backs or beside them), so
that they could cross rivers without breaking rank or losing control
of their steeds and their weapons.[7] Such troops must have been in-
valuable on the British campaigns when rivers had to be crossed in
the face of an enemy. They were probably the auxiliaries used by
the Roman general Agricola in AD 78 during his expedition to the
island of Mona (Anglesey), which Tacitus also records.   The auxiliaries were set to swim across the Menai Straits with their horses
and weapons, and managed to do this so quickly that all resistance
collapsed. The astonished Britons sued for peace, and the Romans
swiftly gained possession of the island.[8]

The military phase of the Roman conquest gave way in due course
to a long period of peaceful occupation.   The role of swimming in
the Roman province of Britain changed accordingly. As we shall see,

the Romans enjoyed the use of water for health and pleasure. Baths,
both public and private, were established in the towns, the military
barracks and the great houses of Roman Britain. These were primarily
meant for sweating, washing and bathing in relatively confined spa-
ces, but a few larger pools appear to have been built in which proper
swimming could be done. The spa towns of Bath and Buxton both had
swimming pools, and a third has been traced at Well in Yorkshire,
which may have been a religious centre.[9] At Wroxeter in Shropshire,
the tribal capital of the Cornovii, an open-air swimming pool has
been identified beside the public baths, though it is not certain
that the pool was ever finished.[10] The Romans can thus be credited
with establishing the first artificial pools in Britain for swimming,
and the only ones until the Industrial Revolution. The number of
pools which have been discovered, however, is small and we should
beware of assuming that such facilities were ever common. Most Roman
swimming in Britain, whether by conquerors or natives, may well have
been done in natural waters—rivers and ponds—as was to be the general
practice down to the nineteenth century. Even at Rome the River
Tiber was a highly popular location for swimming, irrespective of the
artificial amenities.

The nature and significance of Roman swimming do not emerge from
the handful of records relating to Britain alone. For this we must
turn our attention to Rome itself. Swimming occupied an important
place among the activities of Roman society, and this was reflected
in literature.[11] The writings of Rome in the classical era: history
and biography, letters and poetry, include numerous mentions of swimming and supply a good deal of evidence about the matter. They ill-
ustrate the kinds of people who swam, the places in which they did
so, the motives which led them to swim and the status of swimming in
society—in short all aspects of the skill except for the techniques
by which it was done, which alone remain obscure. No Latin author
appears to have written a major work of instruction on the subject.
True, Ovid complains that the multifarious topics on which poets have
written verses include even ball games, swimming and the bowling of
hoops.[12] But his remark, if serious, probably relates to a poetical
effusion rather than a practical or technical treatise. The writing

of a manual on swimming was not to be achieved until the sixteenth century AD.[13]

The literary sources reveal that swimming was widely in vogue among males in Roman society. Women in contrast did not swim, at least not those of elevated rank, and Ovid in his remarks on exercise for ladies in *The Art of Love*, excludes the skill decisively: 'the Tuscan river does *not* bear you down upon its placid stream'.[14] Men, however, were taught to swim in youth or learnt by themselves, and Plautus describes how they did so. 'They lie on a rush float, so as not to work so hard, and so as to swim more easily and use their arms.'[15] Horace, too, mentions the use of cork floats by the young.[16] The skill was more than a peripheral or extra-curricular part of a boy's upbringing. Swimming had high status as a healthy, manly and useful activity; it was thought of as essentially and trad-itionally Roman, and was traced back to the legendary hero Horatius Cocles who had swum the Tiber memorably after defending the bridge against the Etruscans.[17] The great Roman statesman Marcus Portius Cato (234-149 BC) was believed in later times to have personally trained his son Sertorius in athletic pursuits, including 'how to endure heat and cold and to swim lustily through the eddies and bil-lows of the Tiber'.[18] His example may have been in the mind of the Emperor Augustus in about the last decade BC, when he made at least a gesture of giving personal instruction in 'reading, swimming and the other elements of education' to his grandsons Gaius, Lucius and Agrippa.[19] So widespread was the skill among the upper ranks of Roman society that, in the view of Suetonius, it was the inability of the Emperor Gaius (Caligula, AD 12-48) to swim that called for com-ment, not the reverse.[20] The activity was popular, too, among male society as a whole. Young Roman males especially bathed and swam in summer in the Tiber and in the other waters around the city. Ovid recalled them in the springtime, from his banishment at Tomi, bathing their weary limbs in the Virgo aqueduct,[21] and Cicero accused the Roman lady Clodia of having purposely procured grounds near the Tiber, close by the place where the young men came to bathe. One of them, he added insultingly, might make her an offer of marriage.[22]

Swimming in civil society, then, was valued by some as a manly skill and by others as a pleasurable recreation. As society became more highly organised and the standard of living rose, the recreational aspect of swimming developed accordingly. Public baths came to be provided with pools (*piscinae*) in which it could be done, and by the first century AD the most luxurious private houses boasted their pools as well. Pliny the Younger (AD 61-112) possessed one at his sea-side villa in Tuscany: a warm-water pool 'of extraordinary workmanship, in which you may swim and have a view of the sea at the same time'.[23] It is not recorded that the growth of artificial heated pools led to the development of swimming as an athletic sport in the modern sense, with competitions or water games. There may have been impromptu races in the pools or among the young men in the Tiber, but the absence of mentions in literature shows that the idea of the contest never developed far. Rather, Roman swimming was an individualistic activity, with principal reference to oneself. Among some of the wealthiest and most extravagant patricians, individual taste led to swimming of a luxurious and exotic kind. The Emperor Domitian (reigning AD 81-96) was said by Suetonius to have swum with common prostitutes,[24] while Elegabalus (reigning AD 218-222) had his swimming pools strewn with roses and perfumed with their essence.[25] Others disapproved of such practices and proclaimed their allegiance to traditional Roman virtues through the traditional kind of swimming. Seneca the Younger (*c.* AD 1-65) poured scorn on his own times, in which the aristocracy thought themselves poor and mean if their swimming pools were not lined with Thasian marble.[26] He himself, 'a cold water enthusiast', celebrated 1 January with a plunge into the Virgo aqueduct, and swam in the Tiber or in a tank 'warmed only by the sun'.[27]

This dual conception of swimming, luxurious and exotic on the one hand and heroic and manly on the other, is also apparent in literature. Seneca's views are reflected by Plutarch and Suetonius who, as we have seen, took care to record the swimming feats of the men they biographised, when such traditions existed. Virgil too identified swimming in frigid conditions as part of the prowess of the ancient Romans:

> Our hardy race brings its sons to the rivers early,
> And hardens them to the frost and the waters.[28]

In contrast, the legend of Leander swimming to Hero across the Helles-
pont (the modern Dardanelles) was used on other occasions to associate
the skill with love and death rather than heroism and survival. The
story is briefly touched on in this sense by Virgil in the *Georgics*,
as an example of the power of love to spur on its captives to danger
and death:

> What of the youth in whose bones the mighty flame
> Of love is fanned? In the turmoil of rough storms
> He swims the straits, late in the gloomy night.[29]

It was given its fullest treatment in literature, however, by Virgil's
younger contemporary Ovid in his *Heroides*: pairs of letters in verse
supposed to have been exchanged by famous lovers. The letters of Hero
and Leander are imagined as having been written after seven nights of
rough storm have prevented him from crossing the water to meet her.[30]
They include some descriptions of the swimmer: Leander undressing on
the shore, rubbing his limbs with oil, and cleaving the waves with
pliant arms.[31] The coldness of the water is evoked, the swimmer's
weariness as he makes his unending strokes, and the danger to him of
the open sea. As Hero warns him,

> Ships wrought with skill are sunk in the sea;
> Do you think that your arms are stronger than oars?
> What you are eager for, Leander, to swim, the sailors
>   fear:
> Always for them it follows the wreck of their ships.

It is fair to observe that Ovid was not primarily concerned with
writing a poem about swimming, which was secondary to his main interest: the emotions of love, fear and foreboding in two separated
lovers. Nevertheless, in choosing an episode of swimming for this
purpose, he also helped to make the activity memorable. Largely because of his poems, Leander's feat became the most famous swimming
exploit of all in European literature from the Renaissance onwards.

Swimming enjoyed an important place in one other major sphere of
Roman life, and that was in the army. There it was viewed not merely
as an attribute of rare and exceptional men but as a skill which every

soldier should ideally possess. The evidence for the qualities required of Roman soldiers and the methods used to train them comes
chiefly from the *Epitoma Rei Militaris* by Vegetius, a text of which
mention will often be made in this book.[32] It is a late work, written between AD 383 and 395 and dedicated to the Emperor Theodosius I
in the Christian era, but it was based on older texts now lost. It
praises the military practices of earlier times, and seems to be a
reliable guide to what they were. Vegetius stresses the importance
of swimming in the army for reasons such as we have seen in the campaigns of Caesar. It is necessary in crossing rivers when bridges
are inadequate or non-existent, and it is useful too should floods
arise or enemies attack while the army is hemmed in by water. Vegetius reminds the emperor of the tradition that the ancient Romans
had their military training ground, the Campus Martius, beside the
Tiber, so that the young recruits could wash themselves after their
sessions of drill and relax their bodies by swimming in the water.
He argues from this that all the troops ideally, both cavalry and
infantry, should practise swimming in the summer season,[33] and if
their quarters are near the sea or by a river, they should certainly
be made to do so.[34] How proficient at the skill the Roman armies
really were is difficult to say. Individual acts of swimming by notable heroes in war were believed in and recorded. That of the warrior Sertorius, who was said to have swum the Rhone in 105 BC, stands
alongside the exploits of Caesar and that of the un-named soldier in
Britain.[35] On regular campaigns, however, commanders seem often to
have relied on auxiliary troops when swimming was required. Caesar
when fighting in Spain in 49 BC used lightly armed Lusitanians to
swim across the rivers, 'it being their general custom never to join
the main army without bladders'.[36] Hadrian, fighting near the Danube
in AD 118, employed the Batavi for a similar purpose.[37] We ought
probably not to think of every Roman soldier as an accomplished swimmer under fire, but no doubt the army contained a few, and among the
generality there must have been many men able to swim across ponds or
rivers in an emergency.[38]

If swimming contributed something to the art of war, the reverse
was equally true. It was in the military rather than the civil sphere

that most of the greatest recorded feats of swimming took place in
Roman times. War rather than peace developed the skill to the limits
then possible, and produced the counterparts of the records of today.
The swimming feats of the Romans in war were remarkable partly for
the distance covered, partly for the weight of equipment carried, and
partly for the hazards surmounted: wounds, water currents and enemy
fire. The tradition of Sertorius swimming the Rhone was that he had
lost his horse and swam the river quite unaided, though wounded. He
was wearing his breastplate, carrying his shield and opposed by a
strong adverse current, yet he made the journey successfully, 'so
sturdy was his body and so inured to hardship by training'.[39] Caesar's achievement at Alexandria was similarly noteworthy. It was
believed by Suetonius to have extended a long way, though his estimate of 200 paces was probably mere conjecture. The swimmer was
weighed down by impedimenta, perhaps by armour since he had just been
involved in a battle, and he was in danger of enemy action. The
story of Caesar's soldier in Britain seems also to envisage a man in
armour swimming at least part of a watercourse: someone whose own
standard of perfection involved the bringing of his shield back with
him. One of the greatest swimming feats recorded of a Roman soldier
is that of an un-named Batavian auxiliary serving with the Emperor
Hadrian in Pannonia by the Danube in AD 117—a feat so remarkable that
a written inscription was placed to commemorate it near the spot
where it occurred:

> This is I, formerly the best-known on the Pannonian
> shores and the first and strongest among one thousand of
> the Batavi. I was able (how, let Hadrian be judge) to
> swim across the wide waters of the deep Danube with all my
> arms, and while a weapon from a bow hung in the air and
> fell, I transfixed it with an arrow and broke it, I whom no
> Roman nor Barbarian, no soldier with a javelin nor any
> Parthian with a bow was ever able to outdo. This is the
> site; here I have consecrated my deeds to memory in stone.
> Anyone will see whether he can follow my deeds after me. I
> am an example to myself; the first who did such things.[40]

Since we are told elsewhere that the *cavalry* of the Batavi swam the

Danube with their arms in Hadrian's campaign,[41] it seems likely that
the unknown warrior was a rider, crossing the river in armour with
his horse when he drew his bow and shot one arrow at another—a feat
sufficiently striking nonetheless, given the instability of a horse
in river currents. Examples of this kind testify that Roman soldiers could and did swim with at least a partial equipment of arms and
armour. Most were probably auxiliaries on or with their horses, but
a few were Romans who did the feat alone, by their mere skill and
strength as swimmers.

    The literature of Rome reveals a wide variety of swimming, both
with regard to its participants, their purposes and motives, and the
circumstances in which their skill was done. Historians of athletics
possess in Roman swimming a framework of ideas and practices with
which to compare those of later centuries and different societies.
But Roman swimming is of greater historical relevance still, being
not only comparable with later swimming but inseparable from it. The
civilisation of Rome preserved in its writings has been fundamental
to the ideas and institutions of Europe ever since. Just as the
European nations, sooner or later, have all turned to Latin literature as a repository of poetry, history, law and science, so they
have done (albeit on a smaller scale) with regard to swimming. The
mentions of the skill which occur in medieval and Renaissance literature, and the reputation it possessed until at least the seventeenth
century, were largely due to the respect for classical literature and
for the swimming references it contained. In the pages which follow
we shall have frequently to refer back to the Roman authors who
treated of swimming, and shall find them quoted, adapted and used,
again and again, over many centuries.

THE ANGLO-SAXONS

The Roman control of Britain came to an end in the early fifth century. There followed the invasion and settlement of most of the Roman
province by the Anglo-Saxons, and the burial, for two centuries, of
most of the old Roman civilisation under that of new Germanic nations.

As far as the history of swimming is concerned, however, the conquest
of Britain by the Anglo-Saxons merely replaced one people who swam by
another. The records of the skill in Anglo-Saxon England are few,
but they suggest that swimming was both practised and given a status
of honour in society. The Anglo-Saxons originated in north Germany,
and there is no doubt that swimming was in use among the German
peoples in general during the centuries before the settlement of Britain. Caesar himself remarked on the fact in the 50s BC. Describing
the Germani, a people living east of the lower Rhine, he singled out
their hardiness for comment: 'both sexes bathe in the rivers, and
they wear skins or small cloaks of reindeer hide, leaving a great
part of their bodies bare'.[42] So too the Suebi, 'the largest and
most warlike nation among the Germans'. 'They have trained themselves to wear nothing, even in the coldest localities, except for
skins... and they bathe in the rivers.'[43] When Caesar defeated the
Germani and their king near the west bank of the Rhine in 58 BC, most
of the latter were killed, but a very few, 'trusting to their
strength', set themselves to swim the river 'and so won safety'.[44]
Most relevant of all to the Anglo-Saxons is the evidence about the
Batavi: like them a German people living on the edge of the sea, but
settled further to the south west. The Batavi, as we have seen already, were famous for their skill at swimming with their horses and
for carrying their weapons across the water. There are good reasons,
therefore, for believing that the Anglo-Saxons, a shore-dwelling and
sea-faring people, had knowledge and ability in swimming at the time
of their coming to Britain, similar to that of their neighbours to
the south and west.

The principal Anglo-Saxon references to swimming strengthen this
belief. They occur in *Beowulf*, the great epic poem which was probably composed in Mercia or Northumbria (mid or north-eastern England)
during the seventh century, and which survives in a unique copy written in Wessex (southern England) in about AD 1000. The story of
Beowulf concerns events among the peoples of what is now southern
Sweden and Denmark in the fifth and sixth centuries AD. These peoples
were the neighbours of the Anglo-Saxons while they lived in Germany,
and were still remembered by them two or three hundred years later.

The hero Beowulf, who frees the Danes from monsters and becomes king
of the Geats, is characterised as the perfect type of a warrior:
noble of birth, strong, brave, loyal, civilised—and also able to swim.
Three feats of swimming are ascribed to him, each at a different
stage of his life. First, Beowulf himself tells how in his adoles-
cence or early manhood he made a pact with another noble youth,
Breca, later the chief of the Brondings, 'to venture our lives on the
open ocean'. They set off side by side, with swords in their hands
to protect themselves against whales, and Beowulf wore a mail shirt.
They swam the sea together for five days, until storms drove them
apart and Beowulf was attacked by sea monsters. These dragged him to
the bottom of the sea, but his shirt protected him and he killed
seven with his sword; in the end he escaped, exhausted, and was borne
by the tide to the coasts of Lapland.[45] The second episode took
place in Beowulf's maturity, and also concerned monsters. This time
he dived into the dark lake near the hall of the Danish king and swam,
again wearing mail, 'almost for a day'. He reached the lair of
Grendel's mother at the lake bottom, fought and killed her, hewed off
Grendel's head and swam back with it to the shore above.[46] The last
occasion also related to Beowulf's maturity when he accompanied his
lord, Hygelac king of the Geats, in a raid on the Frisians and Franks:
an historical event which can be dated precisely to the year 521.
The raid had a tragic outcome. Hygelac was killed, and Beowulf swam
back from Frisia to the land of the Geats in southern Sweden, 'soli-
tary and wretched', yet with such strength that he was able to carry
with him thirty men's mail coats upon his arm.[47]

     The swimming in *Beowulf* is certainly not presented realistically.
The swimmer is a superman, capable of exploits far beyond those of
normal human ability. He can swim for hundreds of miles along the
North Sea and the Baltic; he can bear enormous weights as he does so;
he can fight with sea monsters on his way, and he can dive and
breathe normally beneath the water for a whole day. We should nevertheless be cautious of categorising these feats as purely imaginary
ones, remote from reality. They are better seen as the abilities of
real people inflated to the superhuman proportions thought proper to
heroes by those who composed and listened to epic poems. Swimming,

as we have seen, was in use among the early Germanic peoples, and will
be encountered again among the nations of Scandinavia in the Viking
epoch. The literature of Rome reveals that swimming with arms or in
armour took place on exceptional occasions, and Beowulf's feats differ
from these not in principle but merely in literary scale. The attribution of swimming to Breca is especially significant, since it shows
that the skill was not associated with heroes alone; it was also something of which other noblemen might be capable. That Beowulf and
Breca swam together, in a kind of contest, is also credible. The
Romans had not emphasised competitive swimming, but the Norse sagas of
later centuries contain several references to contests by two men, and
the *Beowulf* episode seems to belong to the same tradition. In short,
the swimming in the story appears to be based upon real abilities and
practices among the nations of north Germany and Scandinavia, magnified to accord with the requirements of epic poetry. Its presence in a
poem written in eighth-century England and still current when copied
in about the year 1000 also suggests something about its status during
this period. *Beowulf* implies that swimming was both familiar to the
poem's English listeners and respected by them. The skill is presented as a notable part of the hero's greatness, and its reputation must
have benefitted accordingly. The audience of *Beowulf*, if it did not
value swimming already, must have been led to do so by the association
of the activity with such a famous hero.

   The evidence for Anglo-Saxon swimming outside *Beowulf* is scanty,
but it tends to confirm the points which have just been asserted: a
knowledge and approval of the skill. A treatise on dreams and how to
explain them, contained in an Anglo-Saxon manuscript of the mid eleventh century, indicates that people dreamt of swimming since it warns
that to see oneself do so is a token of harm.[48] A poem preserved in the
eleventh-century Exeter Book, on the subject of 'The Skills of Men',
includes the sentence 'some are *syndig*'.[49] This is thought likely to
relate to one of the Anglo-Saxon words for swimming, *sund*, and to mean
'skilled in swimming'. Most telling of all is the evidence of two
Anglo-Saxon translations of Latin works originally written under the
later Roman Empire. The first is the late ninth-century version of
the *Historiae* or world history by the Spaniard Orosius, compiled in

about 418. Orosius describes how Cyrus, king of the Persians, march-
ed with his army to attack Babylon, but was prevented from doing so
by the River Gyges. One of the king's knights, on reaching the water,
felt confident that he could cross it (*transmeandi*), but was carried
away by the river and drowned. The translator of this passage glossed
the word 'cross' (*oferfaran*) with the explanation 'with swimming' (*mid
sunde*), as if he expected that a king's knight would cross in this
way.[50] A similar gloss is made in the Anglo-Saxon prose translation
of the story of *Apollonius of Tyre*, preserved in another mid eleventh-
century manuscript. The Latin text is itself a translation, made between the third and fifth centuries AD, of a lost Greek original. It
tells how, after a shipwreck in the Mediterranean, Apollonius was
driven onto the shore of Cyrenaica 'with the help of a board' (*tabulae
beneficio*). The Anglo-Saxon version completely ignores the board and
relates that Apollonius reached the shore by swimming (*mid sunde*).[51]
Both translators seem to have assumed that noblemen like Apollonius
and the Persian knight could swim, and since the original texts themselves do not demand this assumption, it seems likely to have reflected contemporary practices. The picture accords exactly with the
skills we have seen ascribed to the noblemen Breca and Beowulf.

It remains briefly to mention the swimming of Wales, the only
part of the Roman province of Britain unconquered by the Anglo-Saxons.
The collection of early Welsh heroic and romantic tales, *The Mabinogion*, occurs in texts of the thirteenth and fourteenth centuries,
but the tales themselves may have been put together as early as the
eleventh. They feature a heroic society parallel in some ways to that
of Anglo-Saxon literature, in which practising swimmers may also have
lived. In the tale of *Culhwch and Olwen*, the first surviving Arthurian story, we are told of the deeds of Cei, Arthur's half-brother,
whom later writers transformed into his surly and quarrelsome steward
Kay but who was earlier a more powerful figure. 'Cei had this pecu-
liarity: nine nights and nine days his breath lasted under water.'[52]
This hints at the exploits of a hero like Beowulf, who can dive beneath the sea or into pools and have adventures there. The story of
Math Son of Mathonwy features an explicit swimming hero, Dylan son of
Aranrhod. 'The boy was baptized, and the moment he was baptized he

made for the sea. And there and then, as soon as he came to the sea
he received the sea's nature, and swam as well as the best fish in
the sea. And for that reason he was called Dylan Eil Ton (Sea son of
Wave). No wave ever broke beneath him.'[53] Here too we hear an echo
of a society in which swimming was admired and, perhaps, in use as a
result.

THE VIKINGS

The Norse involvement with Britain began with the sack of Lindisfarne
by Vikings in 793 and lasted until the kings of Denmark and Norway
conceded their rights over the islands of Orkney and Shetland in
1468. It reached its height with the Viking attacks on Britain in
the ninth, tenth and eleventh centuries. The evidence for Norse
swimming during this foremost period comes from the Icelandic sagas
of the thirteenth, which contain accounts of historical events and
family life in the Norse society of the Viking era. The sagas present some problems of interpretation. They were written much later
than the events they profess to describe, and it is often difficult
to separate the practices of the past from those of the times in
which they were written. They also concentrate upon the history of
the Norwegians, who were mainly involved with Scotland, rather than
that of the Danes, the conquerors and colonists of England. Nevertheless, they have a value. Their references to swimming are numerous, so much so as to suggest that the accomplishment was a common
one in Norse society. The evidence gives some idea of the way in
which swimming was practised and the attitudes towards it, to a
greater extent than do the writings of Anglo-Saxon or later-medieval
England. Some of the people to whom swimming is ascribed were historical figures who are known to have visited or to have lived in the
British Isles, including three kings of Norway (Olaf Tryggvason, who
raided England in the 990s, Saint Olaf Haraldsson, who fought there
in the 1010s, and Sigurd Jerusalem-Farer, who visited there in
1108)[54] and two Norse earls of Orkney: Saint Magnus (died 1117) and
his nephew Kali-Rognvald (died 1158).[55] There can be no doubt that,

historically, the Viking expansion brought swimmers to Britain and reinforced, for a time, the native swimming tradition.

The ability to swim is attributed widely to men in Norse literature. As in *Beowulf* it is part of the prowess of the saga-heroes: Skallagrim and Egil in *Egil's Saga* (*c.* 1230, relating to the tenth century);[56] Kjartan and Bolli in *The Laxdale Saga* (*c.* 1250, relating to *c.* 1000);[57] Gunnar and Skarp-Hedin in *Njal's Saga* (*c.* 1280, relating to *c.* 990);[58] and Grettir and Bjorn in *Grettir's Saga* (*c.* 1325, relating to the early eleventh century).[59] It is ascribed to several kings of Norway in the historical saga *Heimskringla*, compiled by Snorri Sturluson in the early thirteenth century, and also to members of the Norwegian aristocracy.[60] Ordinary people are mentioned as swimmers as well. When Kali in *The Orkneyinga Saga* (*c.* 1200, about events a century earlier) wishes to search for treasure in a cave in Norway, the only man who will accompany him is a farmhand named Havard. They swim across an underground lake, 'holding a rope between them, with Kali ahead carrying a blazing log in his hand and a tinderbox between his shoulderblades', but they find no treasure and are forced back by bad air.[61] In *Egil's Saga* the story features three Irish slaves, who escape from servitude and swim from the coast of Iceland to some small islands offshore, and there is even a woman swimmer: Thorgerd Brak, the slavewoman of Skallagrim and the foster-mother of his son Egil.[62] She is clearly an exceptional person, however: a big woman, as strong as a man and a great sorceress who, when chased by Skallagrim to a cliff, is able to jump down it and to swim away. In general the swimming in the sagas, like that of the Romans and the Anglo-Saxons, is confined to males.

The circumstances of Norse swimming are sometimes fantastic and parallel the superhuman achievements described in *Beowulf*. Grettir, the hero of *Grettir's Saga*, dives in pursuit of a predatory troll-woman as Beowulf does after Grendel's mother; on another occasion he plunges behind a waterfall in Iceland and discovers a giant in a cave.[63] In *Egil's Saga* Skallagrim is a smith in western Iceland. Needing a stone for an anvil, he takes a ship upon the nearby fjord, dives into the water and comes back with a large boulder. The saga writer adds that it can still be seen at the site of his smithy,

'with a pile of slag alongside it, and the hammer-marks can be seen
on the top. It has been polished by the waves and there's no other
stone there like it. Four men nowadays couldn't lift it.'[64] Usually, however, the feats are realistic and, like that of Kali in the
cave, present a credible picture of the ways in which swimming was
done. It is performed in all kinds of open water: ponds, lakes,
rivers and the sea. It is done on the surface and, for short distances, underneath. When King Olaf Tryggvason was drowned trying to
flee by swimming after a sea-fight in the Baltic in 1000, some people
believed that he swam underwater and escaped.[65] In summer it can be
done naked; King Sigurd Jerusalem-Farer is described throwing off his
clothes before entering the water.[66] But when long swims have to be
made in the sea, or in times of emergency, clothes are worn for protection. Saint Magnus, earl of Orkney, escapes from the king of
Norway's fleet, while anchored off the Scottish coast, by swimming
ashore in his underwear.[67] Grettir swims clothed on two occasions.
Once he crosses a channel in Norway to borrow fire, dressed in a
tunic tucked into trousers of coarse cloth.[68] Later, he makes his
most famous swim of all from the island of Drangey to the mainland of
Iceland, a distance estimated at four miles.[69] This was considered
to be an exceptional feat, yet it is quite possible for a strong man.
The swim was made after careful preparations. Grettir again wore a
tunic and trousers, and he had his fingers webbed—a rare and valuable
glimpse of an artificial aid to improve the swimmer's range and power.

     Instances such as these reveal the individualistic and practical
sides of Norse swimming. It is often done alone, for purposes of exploration, travel, rescue or escape. It has its place in war, though
in a defensive not an offensive capacity. At the same time it was
also practised for social and recreational purposes. *The Laxdale
Saga* depicts the young Icelanders of a valley swimming together for
pleasure in the Salmon River.[70] Later in the same saga it is described how, 'one fair weather day' in the autumn, men went out of
the town of Nidaros in Norway (the present-day Trondheim) to swim in
the River Nid. Their swimming featured contests: milder counterparts
of the match between Breca and Beowulf, in which the swimmers play-
fully dragged one another under the water, and 'there was one man who

was much the best at the sport'. Kjartan, the hero of the saga, resolved to challenge him:

> Kjartan then plunges into the river and up to this man who
> was the best swimmer and drags him forthwith under, and
> keeps him down for a while, and then lets him go up again.
> And when they had been up for a long while, this man sud-
> denly clutches Kjartan and drags him under, and they keep
> down for such a time as Kjartan thought quite long enough,
> when up they come a second time.... The third time they
> went down together, and now they keep under for much the
> longest time, and Kjartan now misdoubted him how this play
> would end, and thought he had never before found himself
> in such a tight place; but at last they come up and strike
> out for the bank.

The other swimmer compliments Kjartan on the deftness of his swimming, and identifies himself as the king: Olaf Tryggvason, thus
giving the story a happy ending.[71] The reverse is the case in another swimming match recorded in the *Heimskringla*, 'on a day of
beautiful weather and sunshine in Oslo fjord'. It was attended by
King Sigurd Jerusalem-Farer, who appears to have been jealous of his
own superiority in the water. Elsewhere in the saga it is told how
he quarrelled with his brother and co-ruler Eystein over their re-
spective feats at athletics, Sigurd asserting that he could always
drag Eystein underwater when they swam together, and Eystein reply-
ing that he could swim as far and dive as well as Sigurd.[72] At the
Oslo swimming,

> an Icelander, who was among the swimmers, amused himself
> by drawing those under water who could not swim so well
> as himself; and at that the spectators laughed. When
> King Sigurd saw and heard this, he cast off his clothes,
> sprang into the water, and swam to the Icelander, seized
> him and pressed him under the water and held him there,
> and as soon as the Icelander came up the king pressed him
> down again.

The viciousness of the king's behaviour alarmed the spectators, but
at first no-one would interfere. In the end, a sea-captain named

Sigurd Sigurdson swam out and distracted the irate king, allowing the Icelander to escape but at the cost of drawing upon himself the king's severe displeasure.

To conclude, the sagas reveal a society in which swimming was a common accomplishment: as much as among the Romans and more clearly so than with the Anglo-Saxons. It was part of the prowess of a hero, but it was also widely used by lesser men and so natural as to be almost unremarkable. The expert swimmer, not the swimmer, was singled out for special mention. The praise of those who swam and dived well by the saga writers was matched by a precise knowledge of what was possible in swimming and of how its feats were done. Here too it is clear that swimming was not merely practised but well approved of in the Viking world.

References

1. Plutarch, *Life of Caesar*, chapter 49; Suetonius, *The Lives of the Caesars*, book i, chapter 64.

2. Ibid., chapter 57.

3. Plutarch, *Life of Caesar*, chapter 49.

4. Suetonius, *The Lives of the Caesars*, book i, chapter 64.

5. Plutarch, *Life of Caesar*, chapter 16, sections 3-4. In the sixteenth century the un-named soldier was identified with Cassius Scaeva, whose bravery at Dyrrachium is described by Plutarch immediately before this episode.

6. Tacitus, *The Histories*, book iv, chapter 12.

7. Ibid.

8. Tacitus, *Agricola*, chapter 18.

9. A.L.F. Rivet, *Town and Country in Roman Britain*, London, 1958, p 84.

10. J. Wacher, *The Towns of Roman Britain*, London, 1974, pp 50, 366; G. Webster & P. Woodfield, '"The Old Work" at the Roman Public Baths at Wroxeter', *Antiquaries Journal*, xlvi (1966), pp 231-2.

11. The standard account of Roman swimming is by E. Mehl,

'Schwimmen', in *Paulys Real-Encyclopädie der Classischen Altertums-wissenschaft*, ed. G. Wissova & W. Kroll, Supplement, vol. v, Stuttgart, 1931, cols. 847-64.

12. Ovid, *Tristia*, book ii, line 486.

13. See below, chapter 4.

14. Ovid, *Ars Amatoria*, book iii, lines 385-6.

15. Plautus, *Aulularia*, act iv, lines 9-10.

16. Horace, *Satires*, book i, no. 4, line 120.

17. Livy, *Ab Urbe Condita*, book i, chapter 10.

18. Plutarch, *Life of Marcus Cato*, chapter 20, section 4.

19. Suetonius, *Lives of the Caesars*, book ii, chapter 64.

20. Ibid., book iv, chapter 54.

21. Ovid, *Tristia*, book iii, no. 12, lines 21-2.

22. Cicero, *Pro Caelio*, chapter 15 (or 36).

23. Pliny the Younger, *Letters*, book ii, no. 17, line 11; book v, no. 6, line 25.

24. Suetonius, *Lives of the Caesars*, book viii, chapter 22.

25. *Scriptores Historiae Augustae: Antoninus Elegabalus*, chapter 21, section 6; chapter 24, section 1.

26. Seneca the Younger, *Epistulae Morales*, no. 86, section 6.

27. Ibid., no 83, section 5.

28. Virgil, *Aeneid*, book ix, lines 603-4.

29. Virgil, *Georgics*, book iii, line 260.

30. Ovid, *Heroides*, books xviii-xix.

31. Compare Horace, *Odes*, book iii, no. 12, for an episode similar to Ovid's in which a girl imagines her lover swimming up the Tiber.

32. Vegetius, *Epitoma Rei Militaris*, ed. C. Lang, 2nd ed., Leipzig, 1875.

33. Vegetius, book i, chapter 10.

34. Ibid., book iii, chapter 4.

35. Plutarch, *Life of Sertorius*, chapter 3.

36. Caesar, *Civil War*, book i, chapter 48.

37. Dio Cassius, *Roman History*, book lix, section 9.

38. G.R. Watson, *The Roman Soldier*, London, 1969, p 55.

39. Plutarch, *Life of Sertorius*, chapter 3.

40. *Corpus Inscriptionum Latinarum*, vol. iii, part i, ed. T. Mommsen,

Berlin, 1873, no. 462.

41. Dio Cassius, *Roman History*, book lix, section 9.

42. Caesar, *Gallic War*, book vi, section 21.

43. Ibid., book iv, section 1.

44. Ibid., book i, section 53.

45. *Beowulf*, lines 499-581.

46. Ibid., lines 1492-96, 1618-25.

47. Ibid., lines 2359-68.

48. O. Cockayne, *Leechdoms, Wortcunning and Starcraft of Early England*, 3 vols., London, 1866, iii, 212-13.

49. *The Exeter Book*, ed. G.P. Krapp & E. van K. Dobbie, London & New York, 1936, p 139.

50. *The Old English Orosius*, ed. Janet Bately, London, Early English Text Soc., supplementary series, vi, 1980, p 43.

51. *The Old English Apollonius of Tyre*, ed. P. Goolden, Oxford, 1958, pp 16-17.

52. *The Mabinogion*, trans. Gwyn Jones & Thomas Jones, London, Everyman, 1949, p 107.

53. Ibid., pp 63-4.

54. Snorri Sturluson, *Heimskringla: Part I, The Olaf Sagas*, trans. S. Laing & Jacqueline Simpson, London, Everyman, 1964, pp 72, 97-8, 118; *Part II, Sagas of the Norse Kings*, trans. S. Laing & P. Foote, London, Everyman, 1961, pp 277, 298.

55. *Orkneyinga Saga: the History of the Earls of Orkney*, trans. H. Palsson & P. Edwards, London, 1978, pp 80, 101.

56. *Egil's Saga*, trans. H. Palsson & P. Edwards, Harmondsworth, Penguin, 1976, pp 78, 102.

57. *The Laxdale Saga*, trans. Muriel Press, London, Everyman, 1964, pp 103, 132-4.

58. *Njal's Saga*, trans. M. Magnusson & H. Palsson, Harmondsworth, Penguin, 1960, pp 73, 83.

59. *The Saga of Grettir the Strong*, trans. G. Hight, London, Everyman, 1914, p 154; *Grettir's Saga*, trans. D. Fox & H. Palsson, Toronto, 1974, p 122.

60. *Heimskringla, Part II: Sagas of the Norse Kings*, pp 298, 312.

61. *Orkneyinga Saga*, p 101.

62. *Egil's Saga*, pp 201, 95.

63. *The Saga of Grettir*, pp 173-6; *Grettir's Saga*, pp 137-40.

64. *Egil's Saga*, p 78.

65. *Heimskringla: Part I, The Olaf Sagas*, pp 97-8.

66. *Heimskringla: Part II, Sagas of the Norse Kings*, p 312.

67. *Orkneyinga Saga*, p 80.

68. *The Saga of Grettir*, p 106; *Grettir's Saga*, pp 84-5.

69. *The Saga of Grettir*, pp 195-6; *Grettir's Saga*, pp 154-5.

70. *The Laxdale Saga*, p 103.

71. Ibid., pp 132-4.

72. *Heimskringla: Part II, Sagas of the Norse Kings*,   p 298.

73. Ibid., p 312.

Chapter Two

THE MIDDLE AGES, 1066-1500

The Norman Conquest of 1066 brought a new ruling aristocracy to Britain. It was a landmark in the history of swimming, too, in that the Normans were the first conquerors of the island in historic times to whom, we can fairly say, the skill was not very important. The grounds for this assertion will emerge as we continue. Gradually after the Conquest new institutions and forces took root in Britain, which ended by influencing even such an apparently self-contained activity as swimming. First, there was a new kind of military figure: the mounted armoured knight, with new military textbooks to explain and expound his skills. Second, there evolved new kinds of narrative literature treating of physical prowess: the chanson de geste and the romance, which differed from the genres of literature we have encountered so far. Third, the post-Conquest period coincided with new developments in the organisation of the Catholic Church, making this a convenient point at which to consider the relationship of swimming to the Christian religion. It will be the business of the following chapter to examine the literature of these three areas —religion, knighthood and narrative story—in order to see what light they throw upon swimming in Britain from 1066 until about the year 1500. As before, we shall attempt to ascertain the status of the skill, the attitudes of people towards it, and the evidence for swimming in practice: who swam in Britain during the period, and how they did so.

RELIGIOUS LITERATURE

Swimming was known and practised in the Holy Land in both Old and New Testament times. The Bible, however, contains only four clear references to the subject. The Book of Isaiah, predicting the downfall of the people of Moab, compares them with a swimmer, sinking as he stretch-

es out his hands.[1]   The Book of Ezekiel talks of a stream 'deep
enough to swim in',[2] and the First Book of Maccabees tells how the
Jewish commander Jonathan swam the Jordan with his men to escape the
army of the Syrians.[3]   Finally, the Acts of the Apostles, in its account of Saint Paul's shipwreck off the island of Malta, relates how
some men swam from the wreck to safety while others floated ashore on
planks.[4]   The most important of these references, in the history of
biblical commentary and scholarship, was that of Isaiah.   The Ezekiel
and Maccabean references, being brief and casual ones, attracted
little notice, while the swimming in Acts was overshadowed by the
shipwreck: a matter of greater concern to commentators than the swimming which ensued.

The standard medieval text of the Bible was the Vulgate, the
Latin translation made in the late fourth century by Saint Jerome who
based it, in the case of the Old Testament, on Hebrew originals.   The
Vulgate version of the Isaiah swimming episode reads in English as
follows:

> And he shall thresh Moab beneath him,
> As chaff is crushed in a cart,
> And he shall spread out his arms beneath him,
> As a swimmer spreads himself to swim,
> And he shall humble his glory,
> With the dashing of his hands.[5]

The difficulty of this passage lies in the undifferentiated use of
the word 'he'. Jerome and the medieval Catholic commentators upon
him considered that the 'he' who threshed Moab was God, and that the
'he' who spread his arms like a swimmer was Moab. This is the opinion of modern scholars too, but in the sixteenth century different
views were held, as we shall see. The result was to associate swimming in the minds of medieval biblical scholars with ideas of danger,
torment and destruction. This is apparent from the summary of their
writings compiled by the Flemish Jesuit, Cornelius a Lapide (Cornelis
Cornelissen van den Steen) in his great seventeenth-century survey of
Bible commentaries. 'Our /text, the Vulgate/, the Septuagint /the
Greek text of the Old Testament/ and others', says Cornelius,

believe this passage to refer to Moab and to mean that the
demons and all the ungodly will be trampled down by Christ
the Judge, so that they give the appearance of someone who
is wholly vanquished, like the form of a swimmer who, ex-
tending and contracting his arms, displays the gesture of
a man utterly vanquished and in despair.

Thus Saint Jerome, Adam /probably the twelfth-century
commentaries ascribed to Adam of St Victor/, &c., compare
/the ungodly/ with a shipwrecked swimmer in the sea because,
just as such a one is tumbled about in the depth of the
sea, so the ungodly, being shipwrecked from salvation, are
tumbled about in the abyss of Gehenna.... Second, just as
a swimmer in the vastness of the sea spreads out his arms in
every direction like a tree, or grasps a rock by which he
may escape, yet in vain since he finds nothing that he
seizes but escapes him, so the damned catch in vain at a
means of escape from punishment, or an alleviation of it.
Thirdly, just as the swimmer in the sea despairs of life, so
the wicked despair of pardon.[6]

The medieval tradition of commentary summarised here gives a picture
of swimming both pessimistic and unfavourable. The activity of the
swimmer is compared with the fate of the damned. He is not portrayed
with attributes of strength, skill or survival; instead he is shown
at the mercy of the sea, overwhelmed by its power and immensity, denied the means of reaching safety, and finally overtaken by despair.
The image is that of a shipwrecked sailor who swims for a while in
terror and in pain, only to be lost at the end.

Hardly less gloomy is the view of swimming which emerges from
another group of medieval religious writings: the literature of miracles. This is well illustrated by an example from the late sixth-
century *Dialogues* of Saint Gregory the Great, which were well known
in medieval England and translated into Anglo-Saxon in about 900.
The miracle in question was related by Gregory to publicise the
benefits which spring from the consecrated bread of the mass. It is
a story of Agatho, bishop of Palermo, who was going by ship from
Sicily to Rome when one of the sailors, named Baraca, fell overboard

and was presumed lost. On the third day afterwards, the bishop saw a
vision of the sailor as one in danger of death but from whom death
was suspended until the bishop should celebrate mass on behalf of his
soul. He did so, and when the ship reached Rome, there was the sail-
or already. Baraca said that on leaving the ship he had swum with the
waves, and had been sustained by a heavenly visitor who gave him
bread to eat, thus enabling him to reach land. Subsequently the
sailor became a cleric.[7] Parallel incidents can be found in the late
twelfth-century collection of miracles ascribed to Saint Thomas of
Canterbury, murdered in 1170. A young man of Roxburgh is flung from
his horse into the River Tweed, another at Dover falls into the sea
through the capsizing of his boat, and a knight of Perigord throws
himself into water for dread of his enemies. They all experience the
greatest danger in the water and are powerless to save themselves,
until they call upon Saint Thomas and are shortly afterwards delivered in one way or another.[8] Stories like these share the tendency
of the biblical commentaries to depreciate the status of swimming.
They emphasise the danger of man's involvement with water and mini-
mise his ability to survive in the element by his own exertions, even
if he can swim. His survival is due not to his own efforts but to
supernatural intervention, and the role of athlete belongs to Christ,
an angel or a saint, not to the swimmer himself.

References of this kind, however, require to be seen in context.
They represent an element in medieval Christianity, but only one, and
we should not assume from them that the medieval Church or its clergy
took a uniformly hostile or gloomy view of the art of swimming. The
Church indeed does not seem to have ever pronounced on the subject
officially, as it did against gaming and tournaments, and such individual clergy as handled the topic in writing differed in their attitudes towards it. Along with the pessimists whom we have just
encountered, we shall shortly meet two Benedictine monks, John Lydgate and Robert of Reading, who also wrote about swimming with gloom
or dislike. We shall have cause to mention, on the other hand, some
famous clergy who recommended the skill and described it in terms of
approval: John of Salisbury in the twelfth century, Giles of Rome in
the thirteenth, and Jacques de Cessoles and William Langland in the

fourteenth. Swimming was blessed with supporters as well as oppon-
ents in the medieval Church, and in the sixteenth century the first
swimming treatise in Britain was to be the work not of a layman but
of an Elizabethan cleric.

KNIGHTLY LITERATURE

To turn to the knightly literature of the middle ages is to re-estab-
lish contact with the literature of Rome. The basic medieval text-
book of how knights should be trained, do battle and conduct sieges
was none other than Vegetius's work, the *Epitoma Rei Militaris*, which
we have seen summed up the Roman tradition of warfare in the late
fourth century.[9] The *Epitoma* was already attracting the interest of
the Anglo-Norman aristocracy by the mid twelfth century when Geoffrey
count of Anjou, the husband of the Empress Matilda and the father of
Henry II of England, took a text with him to read at the siege of
Montreuil-Bellay in Normandy in 1151.[10] His copy was evidently in
the original Latin, but later on in 1284 a French translation was
made for the better understanding of the aristocracy, and this was
followed by other French versions during the fourteenth century. The
French Vegetius circulated among some of the English nobility during
the later middle ages. One copy, still extant, belonged to a 'Lord
Edward' who was either Edward I or Edward II,[11] another to Thomas of
Woodstock, duke of Gloucester, the youngest son of Edward III in
1397,[12] and a third in about 1450 to Sir John Fastolf, the well-known
English soldier of the Hundred Years War.[13] Finally, in the fifteenth century, Vegetius was translated into English. The first version,
in prose, was made for. Thomas Lord Berkeley and finished in 1408.[14]
Ten copies of it are known, of which one belonged to Sir John Paston
II of Norfolk and another to Richard III or to his wife Anne Nev-
ille.[15] A second adaptation, in verse, was made by a 'parson of
Calais', probably in the late 1450s, and presented to Lord Beaumont,
chamberlain of Henry VI, to be given to the king.[16] It survives in
three manuscripts. There can be no doubt, from this evidence, of the
wide popularity of Vegetius's work in medieval England. What he had

written as a manual for the Roman army was taken up by the medieval
aristocracy as a handbook relevant to their own methods of training
knights and waging war. It circulated widely among them, remained
popular throughout the sixteenth century, and was still being quoted
with approval in England as late as the 1620s.[17]

Vegetius's work, as has been mentioned, included a section on
the importance of swimming, and this was duly reproduced in the medieval French and English translations. The major relevant passage
occurs in book I chapter 10, and is rendered by the English prose
Vegetius of 1408 as follows:

> *How thei mote ben used to swymmynge.*

> Newe chosen knyghtes in somer sesun schul ben taught and
> used to swymme, for thei schol not fynde alwey redy brugges
> over reveres and flodes, bote bothe thei that gon byfore
> and eke thei that commeth after schul be dryven to swymme,
> yif the oost be greet. For ofte tymes the oost, what with
> grete schoures and reynes, what with sodeyn snowes throw
> rysyng and encreesing of ryvers and flodus and unkonnyng-
> nesse of swymmynge, putteth hemself in greet peril, what of
> enemyus on the on side, what of peril of waterus on the
> other side. Therfore the old Romayns, that by us of bat-
> ailles and long preve of periles haddun the craft and the
> ordinaunce of al knyghthood and chivalrie, thei ordeyned
> the feld of chevalrie and us of armes nygh to the ryver of
> Tybre. In whiche the yong juvente of knyghttes after here
> labor and travaille of dedes of armes myght with swymmyng
> wesche awey the swoot and the dust and poudre that thei
> hadde caught with rennyng and ridyng, and also that thei
> myght by cours of swymmyng aslake the feyntise of here
> travaille.[18]

Any medieval knight who read Vegetius, in whatever language, thus encountered a chapter in which swimming was recommended to him as a
practical and necessary skill in war. It was presented as a valuable
part of the education of any youth who wished to become a knight, and
its status was enhanced by its association with the 'old Romayns',
for whom and whose achievements the medieval aristocracy had such

respect. The chapter on swimming, moreover, like Vegetius's work as
a whole, gained even wider currency through its wholesale incorpora-
tion into new works which set out to expound the powers and duties of
kings and knights. It was reproduced by John of Salisbury in the military section of his *Policraticus*, finished in *c.* 1159,[19] and by Giles
of Rome in the 1270s in his *De Regimine Principum*.[20] The latter work,
though written by an Italian for the king of France, circulated widely
in England too in the later middle ages. In 1408-9 the Vegetian
chapter was also incorporated by the French authoress Christine de
Pisan into her *Livre des Fais d'armes et de chevalerie*, and this was
translated into English and printed by William Caxton in 1489.[21]

    Vegetius was the main source of the swimming references in
knightly literature, but there were one or two others. In the *Poli-*
craticus, John of Salisbury quoted Horace approvingly, that those not
able to sleep should oil their bodies and swim three times across the
Tiber.[22] He also inserted into his discussion of military matters
the account by Suetonius of how Augustus instructed his grandchildren
in the art of swimming.[23] The *Policraticus* did not circulate widely
among the aristocracy of medieval England, but the Suetonius passage,
perhaps adopted from John's work, appears in the more popular *Liber*
de Ludo Scaccorum, or 'Book of the Game of Chess', by Jacques de
Cessoles, a French writer of the late thirteenth and early fourteenth
centuries. This work reached medieval England in French versions; it
was translated by Caxton into English in about 1483, and here too
people could read how 'th'emperour Octovyan /i.e. Augustus/ maad his
sones to be taught and lerne to swymme'.[24] Mention may also be made
of the *Disciplina Clericalis* by Peter Alphonsi, a Spaniard of the
early twelfth century who visited the court of Henry I in England and
who wrote his book to explain the behaviour appropriate both to cler-
ics and to knights. Alphonsi declared that a good nobleman should be
instructed in the seven liberal arts, the seven rules for good conduct and the seven knightly skills, the latter being defined as
riding, swimming, archery, boxing, hawking, chess and verse writing.[25] This concept of a sevenfold group of knightly accomplishments,
including swimming, attracted attention in Germany, where it occurs
in Johannes Rothe's work *Der Ritterspiegel* or 'Knight's Mirror'in the

early fifteenth century,[26] but it does not appear to have been influential in England. Few or no other writers adopted Alfonsi's group of knightly skills, and it is not clear that the *Disciplina Clericalis* was known among the English aristocracy to any great extent.[27]

NARRATIVE LITERATURE

The knightly literature current in medieval England certainly included a quota of references in praise of swimming. The popularity of Vegetius's treatise, of the works based upon it and of the *Liber de Ludo Scaccorum* must have brought the notion of swimming into the minds of many medieval kings and knights as something which, in principle, was good for them to learn. How far they put the notion into practice, however, is a separate matter requiring different evidence. Here we can gain illumination from the narrative literature of the middle ages: the stories about the knights and ladies of the ancient world and of Arthurian times, which form one of the main bodies of medieval writings, both in French and English. The first point to note about this literature is that its references to swimming are very few. There are none in the works about Arthur by Geoffrey of Monmouth, Wace or Layamon; none in the famous crusading stories of *The Song of Roland* or the deeds of William of Orange, and hardly any in the romances of Chretien of Troyes. They do not appear in the whole of Chaucer's works or in Gower's *Confessio Amantis*; they are rare in Lydgate, and there are only two in the whole of Sir Thomas Malory's summary of Arthurian literature in the fifteenth century. Clearly, we are in a different world from that of the sagas or the literature of Rome, in which swimming is mentioned with relative frequency.

Such few references as there are can be divided into two categories: those of classical origin, which were taken over by medieval writers as part of the classical works in which they belonged, and those which were apparently invented during the middle ages. Both categories tell much the same story. In the classical group, there are mentions of swimming in the medieval literature of Alexander the

Great[28] and in that of the Trojan War, the latter providing the best
developed example. The medieval stories of Troy, as is well known,
derived from two anonymous works in Greek, translated into Latin during the later Roman Empire and falsely alleged to be eye-witness
accounts of events by Dares of Phrygia and Dictys Cretensis. The two
'authors' describe how one of the Grecian heroes, Ajax Oileus or Ajax
the Little, was shipwrecked off the island of Euboea while returning
home from Troy, with the loss of all his fleet. Dares and Dictys add
simply that, 'after swimming to escape shipwreck, he was drowned, and
others, floating with boards or other aids, perished after they came
to Euboea by being dashed against the rocks'.[29] This brief mention
of swimming was enlarged in the twelfth century by Benoît of Sainte-
Maure in his French *Roman de Troie* of about 1165. Benoît's account,
which is in verse, tells how

> Oileus Ajax the king escaped by chance through swimming, we
> are told, in the dark night. His body was his boat and
> barge; with great sorrow he came to the shore. Many waves
> he encountered before he did so, and so much sea-water did
> he drink that he became full of it: large and swollen. He
> escaped with great peril; face downwards, he lay on a rock.
> ...He had lost fifty of his ships..., their men were lost
> too, and those who saved themselves from death did so by
> their arms and hands, which they made into rudders and
> oars.[30]

This has some original features. It is longer than its classical
sources and differs from them in allowing its hero to reach the
shore, thus building up the swimming into an episode. Its treatment
of the swimmer's plight resembles that of the biblical commentators,
but it does make mentions of his body and of the arms and hands of
his men which display a very faint interest in the swimmer's appearance and movements.

    The episode thus created was reproduced by most of the other
writers on Troy in medieval times. The Sicilian Guido delle Colonne,
whose Latin prose *Historia Destructionis Troiae* (1287) was freely
based on Benoît's work, says of Ajax: 'swimming with the strength of
his arms, he came to the shore half-dead'.[31] The anonymous English

Gest Hystoriale of the Destruction of Troy (c. 1375) improved on this
with:

> Himselvyn in the sea sonkyn belyve,
>
> Swalprit and swam with swyngyng of armys,
>
> Yet he launchet to lond, and his lyfe hade,
>
> Bare of his body, bretfull of water,[32]

where the swimmer is depicted with an appreciative mention of the
movement of his arms which almost suggests his determination. The
fifteenth-century Burgundian writer, Raoul Lefevre, translated by
William Caxton, as *The Recuyell of the Historyes of Troye* (c. 1475),
put it similarly: 'hym self by the forse of his armes and legges,
alle naked swymmyng cam and arryved a lande all swollen of the water
that he had dronken'.[33] The story of Ajax is thus one good index of
the interest of medieval narrative writers in swimming. If it was
already there in their sources they would describe it, and they might
even add a little to it, but only a little and not very often. Indeed, it was possible for John Lydgate, monk of Bury St Edmunds, to
omit the mention of Ajax's movements altogether in his *Troy Book* of
1412-21:

> ...whan his shippes were almost y-drowned,
>
> This goddesse /Minerva/ hath so on him frowned...
>
> That he was fayn for to swymme naked,
>
> As seith my auctor, at meschef to the lond,
>
> And ther he was fonden on the sonde,
>
> Al-most at deth, with-oute remedie.[34]

Evidently Lydgate felt nothing worth saying on the swimmer's behalf.
He was struck only by the unpleasant aspects of the business: 'mes-
chef' or misfortune, nearness to death, and nakedness— a degradation
for anyone, even a pagan king.

The mentions of swimming with a medieval origin point in the
same direction as those from the classical sources. They are unusual;
swimming was rarely attributed to the knightly heroes of the romances
and the chansons de geste, and was indeed seen rather as alien and incompatible with their usual behaviour. The knights of literature went
about their business in armour and on horseback, and authors and their
audiences do not seem to have thought swimming either possible or

proper in these circumstances. A knight who tried it, armed and
mounted, got into difficulties. This is made clear early on in the
history of knightly stories, in Chretien of Troyes's *The Knight of
the Cart* (or *Lancelot*) of about the 1170s. Guinevere has been taken
captive into the castle of the king of Gorre. The castle can only be
reached by two bridges, one consisting of a sword and the other sub-
merged by water. Lancelot, the hero, enters the castle successfully
by the sword bridge, but Gawain (less favoured by French writers)
tries the underwater route. He leaves his horse, lance and shield on
the bank and plunges in, armed with his helmet, hauberk and iron
greaves. At once he is in trouble, for he falls off the bridge into
the stream. 'One moment he rises and the next he sinks; one moment
they see him and the next they lose him from sight.' In the end he
has to be fished out ignominiously by Lancelot and some other knights,
with branches, poles and hooks. He is rescued half drowned with his
body full of water, 'and until he got rid of it they did not hear him
speak a word.'[35]

     Much the same was true later on. The French prose *Roman de
Tristran*, written in about 1230, contains two references to swimming,
both of which were translated and reproduced by Sir Thomas Malory in
his *Tristram de Lyones* in the fifteenth century: the only such references in his works. The first is an unremarkable passage, telling
of Sir Lameroke de Galys,

     that as he sayled, his shyppe felle on a rocke and dis-
     perysshed, all save Sir Lameroke and his Squyer, for he
     swamme so myghtyly that fysshers of the Ile of Servayge
     toke hym up, and his squyer was drowned.[36]

More significant for the author and for us is the second example.
Sir Palomydes is worsted by Tristram in a combat and follows him,
nearly out of his mind with rage, in search of revenge:

     And as he cam by a ryver, in his woodnes /madness/ he
     wolde have made hys horse to have lopyn over the watir,
     and the horse fayled footyng and felle in the ryver, wher-
     fore Sir Palomydes was adrad leste he shulde have bene
     drowned. And than he avoyde hys horse and swam to the
     londe, and lete his horse go downe by adventure.[37]

Like the Gawain episode, this one shows knightly involvement with the
water as a rare and indeed a ridiculous activity. Sir Palomydes is
not a straightforward Christian knight; he is a Saracen, who may be
expected to possess unusual skills. Even so, there is nothing to be
said in praise of his swimming. It comes about through his rage and
negligence, it is entirely devoid of heroism, and it is at best a
desperate expedient. He does indeed escape by it from drowning, but
he is left unhorsed and powerless, and quite unable to pursue his
revenge.

The evidence of the narrative sources must modify the impression
conveyed by Vegetius and the knightly treatises. It shows that in
practice the status of swimming was not very high among the medieval
aristocracy who supplied the characters and the readership of knightly stories. Vegetius's advocacy of swimming may have been respected,
but its impact was evidently limited. The heroes of the chansons de
geste and the romances: Arthur and Charlemagne, Roland and Lancelot,
were rarely or never shown swimming as the heroes of earlier literature had been.[38] This must reflect a decline in the status of the
skill among the post-Conquest aristocracy and its virtual disappear-
ance as a military technique. If medieval knights had swum in warfare, the activity would surely have featured more often and more
honourably in narrative literature than it does. The Romans, the
Anglo-Saxons and the Norse writers had all recorded exploits of swimming by their heroes in time of war, sometimes in armour or on horseback. The literature of the medieval French and English aristocracies
is different, not seeing swimming as compatible with horsemanship,
armour or the use of arms. It is hard to believe, in consequence,
that Vegetius's advice was often put into practice.

SWIMMING IN PRACTICE

If swimming was not regarded as an attribute of the ideal knight, nor
usually part of his technique as a fighter, this does not mean that
no knights ever swam, for pleasure or in need, though they seem to
have done even that less often than their counterparts in earlier

eras. A good illustration of an aristocratic group of men and women
in the thirteenth century, one of whom (but only one) could swim,
occurs in the account of a tragic swimming accident in 1273 recorded
by the chronicler of Lanercost Priory in Scotland, who learnt about
it from an eye-witness: the queen of Scotland's confessor. Margaret
the queen, the sister of Edward I, was taking an afternoon stroll
with her maidens and squires at Kinclavin, Perthshire, on the banks
of the River Tay.

> There was present among the rest a dashing squire with his
> groom, who had been recommended to her by her brother.
> When they sat down on a summit by the shore, he went down
> to wash his hands /in the river/, which he had stained
> with mud while larking about. As he did so, standing up
> and half bending over, one of the maidens, incited by the
> queen, came up behind him unobserved and pushed him into
> the bed of the river. He, making a joke of the thing and
> taking pleasure in it, said, 'What do I care? I can swim,
> even if I go further out.' Thus moving in the river with
> the others applauding him, he felt a whirlpool unexpected-
> ly drag down his body, and shouted and wailed, but he had
> no one who could help him except his servant, who was at
> play nearby. At the clamour of the bystanders, he rushed
> impetuously into the depths, and both men were swallowed
> up in a moment, before the eyes of all.[39]

In the early fourteenth century it was one of the freaks of Edward II
that he enjoyed frolics in the water even in winter, kept company
with swimmers, and may have been able to swim himself. In 1303, when
he was still only prince of Wales, the king's exchequer paid compen-
sation to Robert the Fool for injuries sustained 'through the prince
in the water', presumably in some species of horseplay.[40] Ranulph
Higden, monk of Chester, says of Edward that, 'undervaluing the society of the magnates', he fraternised with 'ditchers, oarsmen,
sailors and others who practise mechanical arts',[41] and this is confirmed by Robert of Reading, monk of Westminster, who tells how the
king took a holiday in the Fens in the winter of 1315-16, to 'refresh
himself with the solace of many waters'. He had a narrow escape from

drowning while 'rowing about on various lakes', and subsequently 'set off at all speed, he and his silly company of swimmers, for the parliament which he had ridiculously caused to be summoned to Lincoln'.[42] Robert's tone is one of disapproval of Edward in general and of his swimming companions in particular. In the fifteenth century Sir Thomas Malory himself may be cited as a knight who could swim at need, at least to a small extent. On Tuesday 27 July 1451, while lying in the keeping of the sheriff of Warwickshire at Coleshill Castle, he broke prison at night and swam the moat to safety—a feat which rivalled in age if not in length the achievement of Caesar at Alexandria, Malory too being fifty years old at the time.[43]

There is evidence too of swimming by ordinary people below the ranks of the aristocracy. London, with its combination of a suitable river and a large population was apparently a main centre of the activity from early times. William FitzStephen's well-known account of London games in the late twelfth century does not mention swimming as such, but he describes water-jousting taking place regularly at Easter, in which young men stood in boats, armed with poles to push one another over. FitzStephen says that the combattants were often knocked overboard and that boats were stationed to pick them up, which makes it look as if such men were at home in the water and could swim or tread water for long enough to survive until rescued.[44] In the early fourteenth century, the English illuminated manuscript known as 'Queen Mary's Psalter' shows pictures both of water-jousting in progress and of swimmers in the water on their own.[45] The poet William Langland, who lived and wrote in London, also portrays men swimming in the Thames in the 'B Text' of his great work *Piers Plowman*, written in the 1370s. This is an appreciative portrayal, praising the practised swimmer and diver against a man of equal size or strength who cannot do so:

'Take two stronge men and in Themese caste hem,
And both naked as a nedle, her non sykerer than other;
That one hath connynge and can swymmen and dyven,
That other is lewed of that laboure, lerned nevere swymme.
Which trowestow of the two in Themese is in most drede?
He that nevere ne dyved ne nought can of swymmynge,

Or the swymmere that is sauf, bi so hymself lyke?...'

'That swymme can nought', I seide, 'it seemeth to my wittes.'[46]

The London swimming tradition was still apparently flourishing in
1425 when 'diverse persons of low estate' gathered on the north bank
of the river to taunt the unpopular Cardinal Beaufort, 'saying that
they would have thrown him in Thames to have taught him to swim with
wings'! This is an interesting threat, since it implies both that the
teaching of would-be swimmers was a familar sight on the river, and
that artificial supports were used for the purpose: analogous to modern 'water-wings' and called by the very same name.[47]

There are a few mentions, too, of swimming elsewhere in Britain:
in rivers (as at London) and in lakes.   Bartholomaeus Anglicus, the
English Franciscan scholar, touches on the skill in his encyclopaedia,
De Proprietatibus Rerum (*c*. 1250), which was translated into English
by John Trevisa in 1398. Speaking of deep holes in rivers caused by
swirling currents, he observes that swimmers are often drowned in
such places.[48] John Barbour in the *Bruce*, his poem on the exploits
of the famous Scottish king, tells how the latter was rowed across
Loch Lomond in a small boat while some of his followers swam behind
him with burdens on their backs,

> For sum off thaim couth swome full weill
> And on his bak ber a fardele.[49]

Later on in 1498 Henry VII rewarded a swimmer named 'Master Griffyn',
perhaps a Welsh squire or the master of a ship, with 6s. 8d. from his
privy purse; we are not told whether Griffyn did feats to amuse the
king or helped in a salvage operation.[50] Popular swimming undoubtedly went on, but it seems to have parallelled the art among the aristocracy in being individualistic and lacking in prestige. The Anglo-
Saxon and Norse traditions of swimming contests appear to have died
out, and this is confirmed by the evidence of the sixteenth century.
Nor did the skill confer much status, even on its non-aristocratic
participants, or make much impact on other people. The narrative
literature of late-medieval England features some popular heroes who
are either commoners or members of the nobility undergoing (for some
reason) a plebeian way of life. They are all shown with physical
skills, but of other kinds. Havelok is a champion stone-caster,

Gamelyn a wrestler, Robin Hood an archer; all are good swordsmen.
None is portrayed as a swimmer, which makes it unlikely that the
skill possessed much status, even among ordinary people.[51]

What swimmers there were in the middle ages, moreover, were also
limited by sex. Even in Norse society, where swimming was widely in
use, we have seen that a woman practitioner was a rare exception.
The possibility of women swimming was conceived of in medieval Britain, but that was about all. The fourteenth-century English
satirical poem, *The Land of Cockaygne*, describes an imaginary country
in which a 'gret fair nunnerie' stands by a river of milk.

> Whan the someris dai is hote
> The yung nunnes takith a bote
> And doth ham forth in that river,
> Bothe with oris and with stere.
> When hi beth fur fram the abbei,
> Hi makith ham naked forto plei,
> And lepith dune in to the brimme
> And doth ham sleilich forto swimme,[52]

but this is mere fantasy. An occasional strong-minded or eccentric
woman may have swum, as we are told of Petronilla, the wife of Arnoul
d'Ardres, a Flemish lady of the twelfth century:

> Frequently during the summer, in the simplicity of her mind
> and through the restlessness of her body, she sent away her
> maidens and descended into the fish-pond in front of her
> knights, with all her clothes off except for a smock or a
> shirt—not simply to wash or to bathe, but to cool herself
> and to move about, along the canals and boundaries of the
> waters, hither and thither, now swimming prone, now supine;
> now hidden beneath the waters, now above them.[53]

The author of this account did not approve of it; he calls the lady
girlish and immature. He shows that a woman was expected to use
water for ablution only, and this was probably all that women did
when they had recourse to rivers or to ponds. Thomas Beckington,
bishop of Bath and Wells, refers to women bathing in the warm waters
of Bath in 1449, but not swimming. The people of Bath, it appears,
were preventing bathers from wearing clothes in the water, perhaps

for hygienic reasons. Instead of the men wearing drawers and the
women smocks, they were all being forced to go naked. The bishop
forbade this practice on grounds of modesty, and ordered that in
future all bathers over the age of puberty should revert to wearing
clothes at Bath, in the traditional manner.[54]

The remaining aspect of medieval swimming which calls for discussion is its visual representation in illuminated manuscripts. In
the absence of any significant writing about how swimming was done,
manuscript illustrations are a possible source for the techniques in
use, though care must be taken in viewing them. We cannot always be
sure that the artists understood the swimming strokes of their day,
and they may have depicted the skill imaginatively or in accordance
with artistic conventions. Only one or two pictures of swimming survive in medieval manuscripts of English origin, but several more can
be added by including volumes produced in France and the Netherlands
—neighbouring and closely related societies.[55] The manuscript
artists agree in showing their swimmers as nude males, in the environment (where this is included) of a river or a pool. The *Très Riches
Heures*, painted for John duke of Berry in France in 1413-16, shows
an actual location: the River Juine by Etampes castle, with one nude
female sitting on the bank, apparently washing herself, while three
nude males swim in the river—the same distinction of the sexes that
has just been postulated. Four of the illustrations show a kind of
breast stroke, in which the swimmer lies prone on the water with arms
extended forwards and legs backwards, both pairs usually a little
apart.[56] This, as it is the commonest, may be termed the conventional treatment of the subject. Three manuscripts show different kinds
of strokes. A copy of the *Treatise on Falconry* by the Emperor Fred-
erick II, illuminated in France by Simon of Orleans in the late
thirteenth century, shows a falconer swimming in a pool, viewed from
directly above. His arms are extended as in the breast stroke, but
his legs are depicted in semi-profile as in the modern side-stroke,
a posture which if not the artist's fancy, may indicate a technique
which combined the two strokes in this way. 'Queen Mary's Psalter'
of the early fourteenth century contains two representations of swim-
ers (fol. 170): one doing the conventional breast-stroke and the

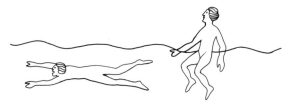

London, Royal MS 2.B.VII, fol.170

Paris, MS fr.12400, fol.115ᵛ

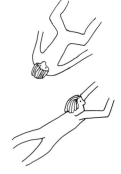

Copenhagen, MS 3384, 8ᴼ, fol.57   *Chantilly, MS 1284, fol.8ᵛ*

SWIMMING IN MEDIEVAL MANUSCRIPTS

(Not drawn to scale)

other standing upright with his body out of the water above the waist.
The latter, whose legs are bent and whose hands are at his sides beneath the surface, is probably meant to be treading water. On the
opposite page (fol. 169^V) stands a man in clothes in a boat, pointing
across the water in the direction of the two swimmers. If he is
connected with them, he must be an instructor or a judge. Finally,
the picture in the *Très Riches Heures* shows a swimmer on his back
with arms outstretched at 45 degrees, thighs extended at right-angles
to the trunk and shins at right-angles to the thighs, in a species of
Old English back-stroke. The manuscripts thus hint at three or four
kinds of stroke, as well as treading water, and considering the scarcity of sources there were probably other strokes in use as well.

The evidence shows that swimming was known and practised in England and Scotland during the middle ages, but not on a great scale
and probably less than in earlier times. It was current in knightly
treatises as an ideal accomplishment, largely because of its Roman
associations, but it was not an attribute of knightly heroes in literature nor often done by knights in practice. It was pursued by
some males among the rest of the population, on an individual basis
and with little reward in terms of prestige. There was no simple
medieval view of swimming except, perhaps, to ignore it. Those who
did pronounce upon it differed in their judgments, some thinking it
dangerous or foolish but others believing it to be useful and praiseworthy. It survived, at any rate, and that was important for the
future. The Renaissance of the sixteenth century was to break new
ground by stimulating the writing of the first treatises on swimming,
but there is nothing obviously new about the techniques they describe,
which seem to be traditional ones. If that is true, what was written
down in the Renaissance was no more than what had been practised in
the middle ages.

References

1. Isaiah, xxv, 11.

2. Ezekiel, xlvii, 5.

3. I Maccabees, ix, 48.

4. Acts, xxvii, 42-4.

5. *Biblia Sacra iuxta Latinam Vulgatam Versionem*, vol. xiii, Rome, 1969, p 107.

6. Cornelius a Lapide, *Commentarii in Sacrae Scripturae*, 10 vols., Lugdunum & Paris, 1875, vi, 284-5. Compare also the medieval comment- aries of Haymo of Halberstadt, d. 853 (J.P. Migne, *Patrologia Cursus Completus: Series Latina*, vol. cxiv (Paris, 1879) col. 838) and of Hervé of Bourg-Dieu, 12th century (ibid., vol. clxxxi (Paris, 1854), col. 243).

7. Gregory the Great, *Dialogues*, book iv, chapter 57; *Bischofs Waerferth von Worcester Übersetzung der Dialogs Gregors des Grossen*, ed. H. Hecht, Leipzig, 1900, section 59, p 347.

8. *Materials for the History of Thomas Becket*, ed. J.C. Robertson, 7 vols., London, Rolls Series, 1875-85, i, 296-8, 316-17, 475-6.

9. On Vegetius's work in the middle ages, see J.A. Wisman, 'L' *Epitoma rei militaris* de Végèce et sa fortune au Moyen Age', *Le Moyen Age*, lxxxv (1979), pp 13-31.

10. *Chroniques des Comtes d'Anjou*, ed. L. Halphen & R. Pompardin, Paris, 1913, p 218.

11. L. Thorpe, 'Mastre Richard, a Thirteenth-Century Translator of the 'De Re Militari' of Vegetius', *Scriptorium*, vi (1952), pp 39-50; M. Dominica Legge, 'The Lord Edward's Vegetius', ibid., vii (1953), pp 262-5.

12. Viscount Dillon & W.H. St J. Hope, 'Inventory of Goods and Chattels belonging to Thomas duke of Gloucester, 1397', *Archaeologi- cal Journal*, liv (1897), p 300.

13. *Eighth Report of the Royal Commission on Historical MSS*, App- endix, part i, section 2 (Darlington, 1881), section 268a.

14. The translation has not been printed; it is discussed in John Trevisa, *Dialogus inter Militem et Clericum*, ed. A.J. Perry, London, Early English Text Soc., original series, vol. clxvii (1925),

pp xciv-xcviii.

15. British Library, Royal MS 18.A.XII; Lansdowne MS 285.

16. *Knyghthode and Bataile*, ed. R. Dyboski & Z.M. Arend, London, Early English Text Soc., original series, vol. cci (1935).

17. See below, chapter 5.

18. Vegetius, book i, chapter 10; text from Oxford, Bodleian Library, MS Digby 233.

19. John of Salisbury, *Policraticus*, ed. C.C.J. Webb, 2 vols., Oxford, 1909, ii, 14 (book vi, chapter 4).

20. Giles of Rome, *Li Livres du Gouvernement des Rois*, ed. S.P. Molenaer, New York & London, 1899, book iii, part iii, chapter 7.

21. *The Book of Fayttes of Armes and of Chyualrye*, ed. A.T.P. Byles, London, Early English Text Soc., original series, vol. clxxxix, corrected edition (1937), pp 35-6.

22. *Policraticus*, i, 47 (book i, chapter 8), quoting Horace, *Satires*, book ii, no 1.

23. *Policraticus*, ii, 13-15 (book vi, chapter 4).

24. Jacques de Cessoles, *The Game of Chess*, translated by William Caxton, facsimile ed. N.F. Blake, London, 1976, fols. B 6-7.

25. *The Disciplina Clericalis of Petrus Alfonsi*, ed. E. Hermes, London, 1977, pp 113-15.

26. Johannes Rothe, *Der Ritterspiegel*, ed. H. Neumann, Halle, 1936, pp 72-3.

27. The work was translated, however, into Anglo-Norman and Middle English: see the edition by A. Hilka & W. Söderhjelm, vol. ii, Helsingfors, 1912, and W.H. Hulme in *Modern Philology*, iv (1907-7) pp 68-9.

28. *Three Old English Prose Texts*, ed. S. Rypins, London, Early English Text Soc., original series, vol. clxi (1924), pp 15, 84-5; *The Wars of Alexander*, ed. W.W. Skeat, ibid., extra series, vol. xlvii (1886), pp 218, 271.

29. Dares of Phrygia, *De Excidio Troiae Historia*, ed. F. Meister, Leipzig, 1873, p 102 (book vi, chapter 1); Dictys Cretensis, *Ephemerides Belli Troiani Libri*, ed. W. Eisenhut, Leipzig, 1958, p 120 (book v, chapter 1).

30. Benoît de Sainte-Maure, *Le Roman de Troie*, ed. L. Constans, vol. iv, Paris, Société des Anciens Textes Français, 1908, pp 244-5,

lines 27,620-41. Dr J.J.G. Alexander kindly informs me of an illustration of Ajax swimming in a 15th-century Austrian MS of the text: Vienna, Österreichische Nationalbibliothek, Cod. 2571, fol. 172^v.

31. K. Sisam, *Fourteenth Century Verse and Prose*, Oxford, 1955, p 228.

32. Ibid., p 74; *The 'Gest Hystoriale' of the Destruction of Troy*, ed. G.A. Panton & D. Donaldson, London, Early English Text Soc., original series, vol. xxxix (1869), p 409.

33. *The Recuyell of the Historyes of Troye*, trans. William Caxton, Bruges, *c*. 1475.

34. *Lydgate's Troy Book*, ed. H. Bergen, vol. iii, London, Early English Text Soc., extra series, vol. cvi (1910), p 792.

35. Chretien de Troyes, *Romans*, vol. iii: *Le Chevalier de la Charette*, ed. M. Roques, Paris, 1958, lines 5096-5128; Chretien de Troyes, *Arthurian Romances*, trans. W.W. Comfort, London, 1914, pp 334-5.

36. *The Works of Sir Thomas Malory*, ed. E. Vinaver, 3 vols., Oxford, 1947, i, 441.

37. Ibid., ii, 535-6.

38. For another knight who swims, but only on horseback with supernatural aid, see *Sir Ferumbras*, ed. S.J. Herrtage, part i, London, Early English Text Soc., extra series, vol. xxxiv (1889), pp 123-4 (lines 3947-64).

39. *Chronicon de Lanercost, 1201-1346*, ed. J. Stevenson, Edinburgh, Maitland Club, 1839, pp 95-6.

40. Hilda Johnstone, *Edward of Carnarvon, 1284-1307*, Manchester, 1946, p 86.

41. Ranulph Higden, *Polychronicon*, ed. J.R. Lumby, vol. viii, London, Rolls Series, 1882, p 298.

42. *Flores Historiarum*, ed. H.R. Luard, vol. iii, London, Rolls Series, 1890, p 173.

43. E. Hicks, *Sir Thomas Malory: His Turbulent Career*, Cambridge, Mass., 1928, pp 94, 103.

44. *Materials for the History of Thomas Becket*, ed. J.C. Robertson, iii, 10.

45. Sir G. Warner, *Queen Mary's Psalter*, London, 1912, fols.

169^V-170 (plates 200-1).

46. Langland, *Piers Plowman*, ed. W.W. Skeat, 2 vols., Oxford, 1876, vol. i: B, xii, 161-70; C, xv, 104-9.

47. C.L. Kingsford, *Chronicles of London*, Oxford, 1905, p 81. *The Oxford English Dictionary* ('Wing', section II. 5b) has no reference to water-wings earlier than the 20th century.

48. Bartholomaeus Anglicus, *De Proprietatibus Rerum*, book xiii, chapter 17; *On the Properties of Things: John Trevisa's Translation of Bartholomaeus Anglicus*, ed. M.C. Seymour & others, 2 vols., Oxford, 1975, i, 663.

49. John Barbour, *The Bruce*, ed. W.W. Skeat, London, Early English Text Soc., extra series, vol. xi (1900), pp 63-4 (book iii, lines 431-2).

50. S. Bentley, *Excerpta Historica*, London, 1831, p 117.

51. The earliest reference to Robin Hood swimming seems to be one of about 1660 (R.B. Dobson & J. Taylor, *Rymes of Robyn Hood*, London, 1976, p 163).

52. R.H. Robbins, *Historical Poems of the XIVth and XVth Centuries*, New York & London, 1959, p 126. Compare *King Horn: A Middle English Romance*, ed. J. Hall, Oxford, 1901, p 82 (L 1431-2).

53. Lambert of Ardres, 'Historia Comitum Ghisnensium', *Monumenta Germaniae Historica Scriptorum*, vol. xxiv, Hannover, 1879, p 629.

54. *The Register of Thomas Bekynton, Bishop of Bath and Wells, 1443-1465*, ed. H.C. Maxwell-Lyte, vol. i, Somerset Record Soc., vol. xlix (1934), pp 116-17.

55. The MSS are: Bibliothèque Nationale, MS fr. 12400 fol. 115^V (French, late 13th century); Copenhagen, Det Kongelige Bibliothek, MS 3384, 8°, fol. 57 (Flemish, early 14th century); Cambridge, Trinity College, MS B.11.22, fol. 121 (2) (Flemish, early 14th century); London, British Library, Royal MS 2.B.VII fols. 169^V-170 (English, early 14th century); Chantilly, Musée Condé, MS 1284 fol. 8^V (French, 1413-16); and Oxford, Bodleian Library, MS Douce 276 fols. 4, 49 (French, late 15th century). For reproductions see Lilian M.C. Randall, *Images in the Margins of Gothic Manuscripts*, Berkeley & Los Angeles, 1966; Sir G. Warner (above, note 45); and *Les Très Riches Heures du Duc de Berry*, ed. J. Longnon & others, London, 1969, plate 9.

56. These are the Copenhagen, London (Royal), Chantilly (duc de
Berry) and Oxford (Douce) MSS.

Chapter Three

THE SIXTEENTH CENTURY

The sixteenth century bears some of the marks of a new era in the history of swimming. More evidence survives about the skill and new attitudes are discernible towards it. Like the Renaissance itself these changes need to be carefully defined, with due regard to the achievements of the middle ages. Swimming was not reborn from extinction; medieval people had both practised and discussed it in writings. The increase of records of swimming is not enough to establish that a growth took place in the numbers or kinds of people who swam, and the evidence of how they did so, as we shall see, suggests the continuance of traditional techniques not the invention of new ones. The innovations of the sixteenth century are really limited to the treatment of swimming by writers, and hence primarily represent changes of attitude rather than changes of practice. First, the educationists of the period include two men (Elyot and Mulcaster) who wrote about swimming at greater length and with more originality than any of their medieval predecessors. Second, in the genres of imaginative literature, references to swimming become more common and constitute, by the end of the century, a significant element in the minds and works of major English writers, again more so than since the Norman Conquest. Third, there appear in Germany and later in England the first specific treatises on swimming. This represents the most original development of all, since it had not been achieved by any previous civilisation in Europe, even by that of the Romans.

NEW INFLUENCES ON SWIMMING

Why did the interest in swimming increase, at least within that part of society embodied by writers and the readers of their works? The question leads us to three other areas of knowledge and ideas which

may have affected the attitudes of people to the skill. First, there
is biblical scholarship and Hebrew studies in particular. We have
seen that one of the elements in the depreciation of swimming by some
medieval writers was its association in the Book of Isaiah with the
downfall of the ungodly. In the early sixteenth century the revival
of Hebrew studies in Europe caused the Hebrew text of the Old Testament to be re-examined by scholars on a wide scale, leading to new
interpretations of its meaning including that of the Isaiah passage.
Whereas Jerome and his medieval commentators had taken the lines

>   And he shall spread out his arms beneath him

>   As a swimmer spreads himself to swim,

to refer to Moab, many sixteenth-century Hebrew scholars, particularly in the Protestant camp, now asserted that 'he' meant God himself,
thus turning upside down the traditional exegesis of the passage.
Swimming, as a result of this new opinion, suddenly became identified
not with the desperate flounderings of the ungodly but with the powerful actions of the Deity. The new interpretation can already be
seen in the first sixteenth-century translation of the Old Testament
into English, that of Miles Coverdale printed in 1535, who based it
on the work of Hebrew scholars in Germany. Coverdale's rendering of
the passage goes as follows:

>   For he shall stretch out his hands upon him, like as a swim-
>   mer doth to swim.[1]

Here the use of the preposition 'upon' rather than 'beneath' shows
clearly that Coverdale understood 'he' to mean God. In the 'Great
Bible', authorised to be read by Henry VIII in 1539, the meaning is
made even plainer:

>   And he shall stretch out his hand in the midst of them
>   (as he that swimmeth casteth out his hands to swim),[2]

and a similar version became enshrined in due course in the 'Authorised Version' of 1611:

>   And he shall spread forth his hands in the midst of them,
>   as he that swimmeth spreadeth forth his hands to swim.[3]

The new translation did not meet with approval in all quarters. The
scholars of the Catholic Church, like Cornelius a Lapide in the seventeenth century, eventually preferred to adhere to the traditional

Vulgate interpretation.[4] In England and Scotland, however, the
triumph of the Reformation meant that for most people the revised
interpretation of the Protestant scholars became the dominant one.

The evidence of the Bible translations is amplified and confirm-
ed by that of the biblical commentators. 'Vatable', says Cornelius a
Lapide, quoting works ascribed to François Vatable, theologian of the
University of Paris between 1530 and 1541,

> Vatable explains this /passage/ in terms of Christ. Just
> as an expert swimmer is accustomed to stretch out and ex-
> tend each hand in order in the water, so Christ strikes his
> enemies (that is to say, the ungodly) with each of his out-
> stretched hands, by the virtue and merit of the cross, on
> which he extends his hands among the ungodly, like a swim-
> mer in the sea, equally with grief and love.[5]

Calvin gives an even more appreciative account of swimming in his
Commentary on the Prophet Isaiah, published at Geneva in 1551 and
issued in English in 1609:

> /This passage/ signifies that the Lord will extend his hand
> into the heart of the region of Moab, not only into the
> outermost parts. Some expound the simile thus. Just as
> the arms are extended in swimming, so the Lord will chas-
> tise the Moabites hither and thither. Others reckon it to
> represent a redoubling of punishment, and by such it would
> be said that the Lord will not only inflict punishment on
> the Moabites once, but he will avenge the cruelty again and
> again which they practised on the sons of God. But we can
> explain the metaphor in a different way. Those who swim do
> not rush forward with a violent motion, but extend them-
> selves lightly and draw apart their arms gently; neverthe-
> less, they cleave the waters apart and overcome them. So,
> often the Lord does not exercise great power to cleave the
> ungodly apart, but overthrows and destroys them without any
> labour or use of large resources, or any noise or tumult,
> however strong and well provided they appear to be.[6]

These views of swimming differ strikingly from those of the medieval
commentators. Vatable likens Christ to a swimmer, talks of the

'expert' and imagines him making his strokes in an orderly sequence.
Calvin evokes the swimmer's ease in the water, his buoyancy, his
ability to 'overcome' the waves, and the care and effect with which
he applies his arms. The tone is one of approval, even of admiration,
and the old associations of weakness, frustration and failure are replaced by those of strength, skill and success. It is tempting to
emphasise what has occurred—and yet the temptation should be resist-
ed. As in the middle ages, it is dangerous to exaggerate the influence of a single passage of literature, even a biblical one. None of
the other writings on swimming in sixteenth-century Britain refer to
the passage concerned, and their authors were probably unaware of its
significance. On the whole the alterations of religion during the
century do not seem to have had a direct effect upon swimming, and
the changes in the interpretation of Isaiah appear to have coincided
with (or reflected) the growth of interest in the skill, rather than
to have caused it.

The second area of potential importance for swimming was the
overseas expansion of the sixteenth century. The expansion, with its
voyages of exploration, trade and settlement brought Europeans into
contact with nations in the tropics where swimming was practised more
widely and to a higher level than in northern Europe. This might be
expected to have stimulated a greater interest in swimming and its
possibilities by the voyagers and ultimately by their countrymen at
home. Swimmers and divers were certainly noticed by English travellers of the sixteenth century. Sir Richard Guylforde, sailing from
the Holy Land to Venice in 1506, describes how the rudder of his ship
was mended at 'Lesyna' (the modern island of Hvar in the Adriatic) by
a diver who went underwater for the purpose nine or ten times because
of the turbulent seas.[7] Francis Fletcher in his narrative of Drake's
voyage round the world relates how *The Golden Hind* was attacked by
natives who could swim in the Pacific Ocean in 1579. When Drake com-
manded a gun to be shot off to frighten them,

> at the noise thereof they every one leapt out of his canoe
> into the water, and diving under the keel of their boats,
> stayed them from going any way until our ship was gone a
> good way from them.[8]

Sir Walter Raleigh, too, mentions an incident during his voyage up
the River Orinoco in 1596 in which his Indian pilot was attacked by
other Indians at the mouth of the river and swam successfully to
safety on the ship, although 'half dead with fear'.[9] In the end,
however, it is as hard to identify an important influence on British
swimming from this direction as it is from the Book of Isaiah. Eng-
lishmen had long taken an interest in the further parts of the world.
In the thirteenth century Matthew Paris described the Tartars as
cruel, blood-drinking horsemen 'able to swim and to sail',[10] and in
the fourteenth the fictitious *Travels of Sir John Mandeville* told of
natives 'all skinned with rough hair as a rough beast' who 'go as
well under the water of the sea as they do above the land all dry,
and they eat both flesh and fish all raw'.[11] Native swimmers were
therefore known or imagined in the middle ages, but of a too remote
and outlandish kind to have any implications for Europeans. Sixteenth-century writers were better informed about the world than
Matthew Paris or 'Mandeville', but their attitudes to savage peoples
had altered little. They too saw tropical swimmers as members of
far-removed civilisations, deficient in religion, society and technology, and native swimming consequently made little impact. We have
to wait until the late seventeenth and eighteenth centuries in England to find notably favourable accounts of the skill, and the savage
swimmer portrayed with real approval.[12]

The third area relevant to the history of swimming was that of
classical studies. This was indubitably more important than either
of the others. It was the developments here, rather than in theology
or exploration, that stimulated a greater interest in the skill among
sixteenth-century writers. This can easily be seen from the literature of the period which deals with swimming. When authors expound
its importance, they do so not with references to the Bible or to
tropical natives but with quotations from classical Latin literature,
a wider range of which was now available than had been known during
the middle ages. This process had been going on in Italy since the
mid fifteenth century, when several writers, notably Guarino da Verona, are found recommending swimming on the grounds of its usage by
heroes of ancient Rome.[13] It first appears in England in Thomas

More's *Utopia* (published 1516-17). In this account of an imaginary
country in the New World, More describes how the 'armature or harness'
(meaning the armour) of its inhabitants

> is sure and strong to receive strokes and handsome for all
> movings and gestures of the body, in so much that it is not
> unwieldy to swim in. For in the disciplines of their war-
> fare, among other feats, they learn to swim in harness.[14]

This is probably not, as might appear, inspired by stories of swimming by New-World natives. In the context of swimming references in
the sixteenth century, it is much more likely to be based on More's
acquaintance with the classics and on the swimming in armour by
Caesar and Horatius, mentioned by Plutarch and Livy. More is ascrib-
ing to the Utopians the excellence which the Romans achieved in the
matter. Two years after More's work, in 1519, William Horman, some-
time headmaster of Eton and Winchester, published his *Vulgaria*:
sentences for boys to translate in schools from English to Latin, and
based in the main upon aspects of everyday life. Two of the sentences mention swimming:

> Children do learn to swim leaning upon the rind of a tree,
>   or cork.
>
> Learn to swim without a cork.[15]

Horman may well have watched the boys of Eton swimming in the nearby
Thames. At the same time, he too was probably recalling the literature of Rome. Plautus observes in the *Aulularia* that boys learn to
swim by leaning on a rush float,[16] and Horace remarks in the *Satires*
that an adult needs no cork to help him swim.[17] The example reminds
us of two truths. Sixteenth-century swimming was an ancient tradition in Britain, and as such might be noticed and appreciated by
contemporary writers. Their notice and appreciation, however, were
enhanced and increased by their reading of the classics and of the
swimming references they found there. These helped to turn their
attention to contemporary swimming and gave it a higher value in
their minds because of its Roman associations.

EDUCATIONAL   LITERATURE

The mentions of swimming in sixteenth-century literature occur, like
those of the middle ages, in two genres in particular: educational
treatises and imaginative writings. The educational literature of
Tudor England had a good deal in common with its medieval antecedents,
the treatises on knighthood, most of it being still primarily directed at the same audience: the nobility and gentry. Vegetius, too,
remained current. A new translation into English by John Sadler was
published in 1572 which reproduced all the original swimming references, including the exhortation that soldiers should all be practised in the skill. 'It is very necessary that not alone the footmen
be able to swim, but also the horses themselves, yea, and the
pages.'[18] 'Horses' here mean knights or cavalry, as well as their
steeds.[19] Besides Vegetius there are recommendations of swimming in
four of the principal treatises written by sixteenth-century authors.
These are *The Governor* by Sir Thomas Elyot (1531), Castiglione's *Book
of the Courtier* translated by Sir Thomas Hoby (1561), *The Schoolmaster* by Roger Ascham (1570) and Richard Mulcaster's *Positions* (1581).
Two of these, Castiglione and Ascham, can be dismissed shortly because
they mention swimming only casually. Castiglione associates it with
leaping, running and stone-casting. He advocates it partly for its
profit in war, as the medieval writers had done, and partly in order
to acquire reputation, 'especially among the multitude'—a new and
uncommon opinion.[20] Ascham refers to it in passing as one of sixteen
activities 'containing either some fit exercise for war and some
pleasant pastime for peace' and therefore 'not only comely and decent
but also very necessary for a courtly gentleman to use'.[21] He does
not say anything about swimming itself, however, and it is not therefore clear whether his attitude to it marked any advance on that of
the middle ages.

   Elyot and Mulcaster, in contrast, treat of swimming at greater
length and with more originality. Elyot links it with wrestling, running and riding in a chapter entitled 'Exercises whereby should grow
both recreation and profit', but he gives it five pages, the greatest
coverage of the four activities.[22] He begins by asserting what was

probably true, that 'it hath not been of long time much used, especially among noblemen', and anticipates that some of his readers will
have little regard for the skill. In recognising this situation and
seeking to reverse it, he adopts the position of a revivalist of
swimming, the first such whom we have met with in the history of
Britain. Elyot's attitude to the skill, like his book as a whole, is
partly derived from the middle ages and partly of the Renaissance.
He starts his account by quoting Vegetius on how the Romans swam in
the Tiber after their military training in the Campus Martius, but
he follows this with five new examples of swimming in classical
times, taken from Livy, Plutarch and Suetonius, which mark an advance
on previous English writers. He is still medieval in seeing the
primary use of swimming as survival 'in extreme danger of wars' and
his classical illustrations are also of military swimming. He does
reveal, however, a secondary interest that is new: the notion of
swimming as an aid to health. The title of his chapter mentions
'recreation' as well as profit, his Vegetius reference touches on
washing and refreshment, and he talks of the 'health' as well as the
'safeguard' which knowledge of swimming brings. When he wrote *The
Governor*, Elyot had transcribed passages from the Roman *Historia
Augusta* which he later published in 1540, telling how the Emperor
Alexander Severus used a swimming bath to wash and take exercise
in.[23] Here too the idea of swimming for health appears to have
entered Elyot's mind, though it did not receive very great emphasis
in his writings.

    Elyot's originality was exceeded by Mulcaster, whose chapter on
swimming in *Positions* gave to the skill the fullest treatment it had
yet received in print in Britain.[24] The elements of Mulcaster's work
are similar to those of Elyot's, but they are present in different
proportions. There is the adoption of a revivalist position: swimming was once 'both in great use and of great price' and ought to be
valued again. There are the classical quotations, not here from
Vegetius but from Livy and Plutarch as in Elyot and also from Ovid.
The same uses of swimming are proposed: its military application
('to assail enemies by water') and its benefits for health, but there
is far more about the second than the first, the opposite of Elyot.

Mulcaster discusses the advantages of swimming to the body, and also the dangers. In hot water it warms and makes nimble the joints, but troubles the head, weakens the body and disperses the humours without dissolving them. In cold water it strengthens the natural heat and improves the digestion, but harms the sinews and the hearing if the swimmer stays in too long. Swimming in salt water is good for head-aches, dropsies, scabs, scurf, smallpox and leprosies, but all swim-ming is bad for the head 'considering the continual exhalation which ascendeth still from the water'. Here Mulcaster is original in another way, since he discusses for the first time in Britain the best locations for swimming to be done. Marsh waters and pools are bad, for they infect the head and body. Lakes and standing meres offer 'reasonable good swimming'; 'the larger they be and the clean-er, the more commodious and wholesome to swim in'. Running rivers are good for those who are healthy, but in fresh water care must be taken of cramp. Best of all is the sea, because salt water is more buoyant and there is least danger of drowning. Such praise of the sea is rare indeed between the Norman Conquest and the eighteenth century. The chapter concludes with a decisive approval of the skill. When supervised by a wise schoolmaster, it is suitable to be taught to children, and its mastery by them is beneficial to the commonwealth. More than anyone since the Conquest, Mulcaster pro-pounded the cause of swimming as a useful and healthy skill in time of peace, thus venturing onto the field which was to be more fully explored by Everard Digby, six years later in 1587.

IMAGINATIVE LITERATURE: SPENSER, MARLOWE AND SHAKESPEARE

The growth of interest in swimming by educational writers was paral-lelled in the imaginative literature of the last twenty years of the sixteenth century. By 1600 literary references to it had become more common than at any time since the Conquest, and it was being mention-ed by leading writers, not simply in passing but as the focus of new and positive attitudes. As in medieval times, but on a larger scale, there was a range of opinions about it, the extent of which can be

seen by comparing the works of Spenser, Marlowe and Shakespeare.
Spenser had particular opportunities to gain an interest in swimming.
He was a pupil at the Merchant Taylors' School in London while Mulcaster was headmaster of it, and he was a junior contemporary of
Everard Digby the writer on swimming at Cambridge during the 1570s.
It is likely that Spenser and Digby had associates in common, and it
has been suggested that the swimming references in the fifth book of
Spenser's *Faerie Queene* (1596) reflect the publication of Digby's
swimming treatise in 1587.[25] In fact, Spenser's literary portrayal
of swimming has as much in common with that of the medieval romances
as with anything that was new in the sixteenth century. We have seen
how Chretien and Malory twice portrayed knights in the water in ludi-
crous circumstances. The same is true of *The Faerie Queene*. In book
two, Pyrochles attempts to drown himself through vexation after being
worsted in combat with Guyon. He jumps into a lake, but is held up
and preserved by the waters which are very thick and muddy.[26] In
book six, Calepine wades across the waters of a ford while the Lady
Serena whom he is guarding sits on his horse. He is insulted by
Turpine, a churlish knight, who 'laughed and mocked to see him like
to swim', and although Turpine subsequently suffers for his rudeness,
the impression remains that knights in the water easily render themselves ridiculous, to their enemies if not to their readers.[27]

    The main swimming episode in *The Faerie Queene* takes place in
the course of book five.[28] Pollente, a Saracen knight, guards a
bridge at which he exacts toll from travellers and offers battle to
all knightly comers. The bridge contains trap-doors through which
the latter fall, after which Pollente leaps into the water on horseback and despatches them, 'through practice usual'. When Artegall
the hero tries the bridge, he too falls into the river with Pollente
in hot pursuit. The two knights remain in their saddles and fight on
the river while their horses swim beneath them. At length Artegall
seizes Pollente's iron collar and Pollente leaves his horse's back.
Artegall does the same and both swim freely in the water:

           So Artegall at length him forced forsake
           His horse's back for dread of being drowned,
           And to his handy swimming him betake.

> Eftsoons himself he from his hold unbound,
>
> And then no odds at all in him he found,
>
> For Artegall in swimming skilful was,
>
> And durst the depth of any water sound.
>
> So ought each knight, that use of peril has,
>
> In swimming be expert through water's force to pass.
>
> (Book v, canto ii, verse 16)

In the end Artegall proves 'better breathed' than Pollente, who flees
to the bank. Artegall pursues him, holding his sword, and kills him
on the land. Spenser is certainly of the new age here in featuring a
knightly hero who can swim, and in allowing him to do so without rid-
icule. His reference to the sword is probably inspired by classical
literature, too, in which swimming with weapons is mentioned. At the
same time, Pollente recalls to us that other swimming Saracen knight,
Palomydes in Malory, and Spenser's final adjuration to knights to
swim is no more than a restatement of the Vegetian tradition. There
is nothing in Spenser which specifically relates either to Mulcaster
or to Digby, and his work could easily have been written without having known about either of them.

Marlowe went up to Corpus Christi College, Cambridge, in 1580
while Digby was still in residence at St John's College, and took his
MA degree in 1587, the year that Digby published his swimming treatise. No connection is known between the two men but, as we shall
see, swimming was practised in late Elizabethan Cambridge and Marlowe
was probably aware of the skill while he was living there, either
from his reading of the classics or from first-hand experience.
There are swimming references in his earliest play, *Dido, Queen of
Carthage*, parts of which were composed not later than 1588 and with
some likelihood in Marlowe's Cambridge years.[29] In the play, Aeneas
the hero tells the court of Dido how he tried to save Polixena from
the Greeks when Troy was sacked:

> I leapt into the sea,
>
> Thinking to bear her on my back aboard,
>
> For all our ships were launched into the deep,
>
> And as I swam, she standing on the shore

> Was by the cruel Myrmidons surprised.
>
>   (Act ii, scene 1, 283-7)

The significance of this passage is that Marlowe's classical sources,
Virgil's *Aeneid* and Ovid's *Metamorphoses*, do not mention Aeneas swimming on this occasion, and although several swimmers are mentioned in
the *Aeneid*, Aeneas is not among them. The attribution was therefore
Marlowe's own and shows, as does the case of Artegall in Spenser, how
much more natural it had become to make one's hero a swimmer than it
had been in the middle ages. This incident is heroic, but later in
the play we can see the associations developing which most character-
ise Marlowe's treatment of swimming: those of love and eroticism.
When Dido realises that her lover Aeneas has deserted her, she cries

>   I'll make a prayer unto the waves
>   That I may swim to him like Triton's niece:
>   O Anna, fetch Orion's harp,
>   That I may 'tice a dolphin to the shore
>   And ride upon his back unto my love.
>
>   (Act v, scene 1, 246-50)

The associations reappear in a later play, *Edward II*, where swimming
is made to express the love of Gaveston for his friend the king:

>   Sweet prince, I come; these, these thy amorous lines
>   Might have enforced me to have swum from France,
>   And like Leander gasped upon the sands.
>
>   (Act i, scene 2, 6-8)

The image of the male body in the water had a special appeal for
Marlowe. It is developed later in the same speech in the fantasy of
the

>   lovely boy in Dian's shape,
>   With hair that gilds the water as it glides,
>   Crownets of pearl about his naked arms,
>   And in his sportful hands an olive-tree
>   To hide those parts which men delight to see,
>
>   (ibid., 60-5)

who 'bathes him in a spring', and it is given an extended treatment
in Marlowe's poem *Hero and Leander*, inspired by Ovid's *Heroides* and
presumably a late work since it was left unfinished at his death in

1593. Like Ovid, Marlowe evokes Leander undressing on the shore and
leaping into the water in the cause of love; but to a greater extent
even than Ovid he portrays Leander's body erotically, not merely by
describing it but by having Neptune accost Leander in homosexual em-
braces as he swims:

> He watched his arms, and as they opened wide,
> At every stroke betwixt them would he slide
> And steal a kiss, and then run out and dance,
> And as he turned cast many a lustful glance,
> And threw him gaudy toys to please his eye,
> And dive into the water and there pry
> Upon his breast, his thighs and every limb,
> And up again and close beside him swim
> And talk of love.
>
> (Sestiad ii, 183-91)

Here for the first time in Britain since the Romans, swimming is depicted in a sensuous way quite different from the military and
practical terms which dominated most writing about the subject, even
in the sixteenth century.

The interest of Marlowe in swimming was equalled by that of
Shakespeare, though they took very different forms. Shakespeare's
works contain a dozen significant references to the subject as well
as casual ones, across the whole chronological span of his writings,
and though they only amount to a minor theme of his work as a whole,
they show that swimming occupied a significant place in his mind, one
to which he returned again and again. His attitude to the skill,
however, contrasted sharply with that of Marlowe in being almost
uniformly hostile and pessimistic, with only one major exception to
prove the rule. True, there are times when the poet, at first sight,
appears to portray swimming as an heroic activity with images of
strength and valour. Hotspur's speech in *I Henry IV* (*c.* 1597) is
such an example:

> By heaven, methinks it were an easy leap
> To pluck bright honour from the pale-faced moon,
> Or dive into the bottom of the deep,
> Where fathom-line could never touch the ground,

> And pluck up drowned honour by the locks.
>
> > (Act i, scene iii, 199-203)

So is the challenge of Troilus to Diomed in *Troilus and Cressida* (*c.* 1602):

> Fly not, for should'st thou take the River Styx
> I would swim after.
>
> > (Act v, scene 4, 20-1)

At the same time, these images of swimming as a powerful, superhuman activity are weakened by the hyperbole in which they are set. Hotspur is rash and Troilus desperate when they utter their swimming fantasies, and neither is described swimming successfully in reality, as Marlowe depicts Aeneas. On the one occasion when Shakespeare had to deal with a character historically attested as an heroic swimmer, he distorted the fact and devalued it. In *Julius Caesar* (*c.* 1599), Cassius tells Brutus how,

> once, upon a raw and gusty day,
> The troubled Tiber chafing with her shores,
> Caesar said to me, 'Dar'st thou, Cassius, now
> Leap in with me into this angry flood
> And swim to yonder point?' Upon the word,
> Accoutred as I was, I plunged in
> And bade him follow; so indeed he did.
> The torrent roared and we did buffet it
> With lusty sinews, throwing it aside
> And stemming it with hearts of controversy,
> But ere we could arrive the point proposed,
> Caesar cried 'Help me, Cassius, or I sink!'
> I, as Aeneas our great ancestor
> Did from the flames of Troy upon his shoulder
> The old Anchises bear, so from the waves of Tiber
> Did I the tired Caesar.
>
> > (Act i, scene ii, 99-114)

Shakespeare has started here with the historical fact that Caesar could swim, but he has turned this into an imaginary and unhistorical episode of a swimming contest between Caesar and Cassius. As in the cases of Troilus and Hotspur it begins with bravado (Caesar's

challenge), and at first all seems to go well. The strength and movement of the swimmers' arms are mentioned appreciatively in terms
resembling the medieval portrayal of Ajax, but not for long. Exhilar-
ation is replaced by one dark image after another: first 'controversy'
——the rivalry of the two men, then Caesar's cry for help and finally
his physical collapse. The would-be victor at swimming is overwhelmed
by the waves and has to be rescued by his rival, revealing a weakness
that Cassius never forgets.

There hovers, then, about these lively representations of swimming a sense of bravado, rashness and danger. In most of the rest of
Shakespeare's canon even the elements of youth and power are missing,
and the associations are entirely gloomy ones. As the following ex-
racts show, the poet's most common portrayal of swimming is not in
terms of strength or beauty but of frustration, fatigue and the ever-
present likelihood of drowning:

> Say you can swim——alas! 'tis but a while!
> Tread on the sand——why, there you quickly sink;
> Bestride the rock——the tide will wash you off,
> Or else you famish; that's a threefold death.
>> (*3 Henry VI*, Act v, scene 4, 29-32)
> Like an unpractised swimmer plunging still,
> With too much labour drowns for want of skill.
>> (*The Rape of Lucrece*, 1098-9)
>> Doubtful it stood,
> As two spent swimmers that do cling together
> And choke their art.
>> (*Macbeth*, Act i, scene 2, 7-9)
> Alas! the seas hath cast me on the rocks,
> Washed me from shore to shore, and left me breath
> Nothing to think on but ensuing death.
>> (*Pericles*, Act ii, scene 1, 5-7)
>> I have ventured
> Like little wanton boys that swim on bladders,
> This many summers in a sea of glory,
> But far beyond my depth; my high-blown pride
> At length broke under me and how has left me

> Weary and old with service, to the mercy
> Of a rude stream that must for ever hide me.
>
> *(Henry VIII*, Act iii, scene 2, 358-64)

The sequence can even be traced in *The Two Noble Kinsmen*, attributed
jointly to Shakespeare and to John Fletcher in the printed edition
of 1634, thus giving extra weight to the attribution:

> Weak as we are, and almost breathless swim
> In this deep water. Do you but hold out
> Your helping hands, and we shall tack about
> And something do to save us.
>
> (Prologue, 24-7)
>
> for not to swim
> I' th' aid o' th' current were almost to sink,
> At least to frustrate striving; and to follow
> The common stream, 'twould bring us to an eddy
> Where we should turn or drown.
>
> (Act i, scene 2, 7-11)

In short, the general treatment of swimming in these passages is at
best cynical and on most occasions pessimistic.

The one major exception to this rule is that of *The Tempest*.
Here alone does the author vary his treatment significantly and
feature swimmers surmounting the water in triumph and unscathed. Of
the passengers on Alonso's ship when it founders off Prospero's island, Stephano floats ashore on a barrel, Trinculo 'swims like a
duck' and Ferdinand is described surpassing the waves in the one
great evocation of the swimmer's prowess in the whole of Shakespeare's
work:

> I saw him beat the surges under him,
> And ride upon their backs; he trod the water,
> Whose enmity he flung aside, and breasted
> The surge most swoll'n that met him; his bold head
> 'Bove the contentious waves he kept, and oared
> Himself with his good arms in lusty stroke
> To the shore, that o'er his wave-worn basis bowed,
> As stooping to relieve him. I not doubt

He came to land.

(Act ii, scene 1, 120-9)

This picture, followed by that of Ferdinand

sitting upon a bank

Weeping again the king my father's wrack,

(Act i, scene 2, 392-3)

is in the tradition of Apollonius and Ajax, and may owe something to
them. But the storm in *The Tempest* is a magic not a real one. The
shipwreck is arranged by Prospero, by whom the usual nature of the
sea is changed and subdued, so that all in the ship may land in
safety. It requires nothing less than supernatural conditions for
Shakespeare's swimmers to survive unharmed. On normal occasions the
fate of a man or woman in the water fills him with fear and anxiety.
Either he must have experienced some dreadful swimming accident, at
first or second hand, which left an indelible scar, or else he adopted the pessimistic views about swimming of some of the medieval
writers. Whatever the case, he stands apart from the simplistic
approvals of swimming expressed by most of the writers of the period.

SWIMMING   IN   PRACTICE

Compared with the views of the writers, there is still only scanty
evidence for the practice of swimming in the sixteenth century. It
is impossible to estimate the popularity of the skill and consequently to ascertain whether that popularity was growing. As in the
middle ages, there are signs that the skill was in use among some of
the aristocracy, especially those who were active in war. Sir Thomas
Chaloner was a young man of twenty in 1541 when, accompanying the
expedition of the Emperor Charles V against Algiers, the galley in
which he was sailing was wrecked in the sea. It is later described
how he swam in the water for a long time until, when his strength had
nearly failed him, he managed to clamp his jaws on a cable thrown out
from a neighbouring vessel and was saved, not without losing some of
his teeth.[31] His contemporary, Sir John Luttrell of Dunster in Somerset, may well have been a swimmer too in view of the striking

portrait of him, dated 1550, which shows him in the sea escaping from shipwreck.[32] The portrait is in part an allegorical representation of man's search for peace from the storms of life, but it is also a remarkable evocation of the physical power of man in the water. It shows the naked torso of Sir John rising upright from the waves at waist height; he brandishes his right arm in the air with a defiant gesture while his left descends beneath the surface. His general posture has some resemblance to a modern swimmer treading water. Chaloner and Luttrell were both members of the English expedition to Scotland in 1547, and it is tempting to speculate that they exchanged their experiences of swimming at that time. Whatever the case, the power of the Luttrell portrait is undeniable and anticipates by a generation the literary parallels to it in the works of Marlowe and Shakespeare.

Further examples of aristocratic swimmers survive from the end of the century. Sir John Pakington, who frequented the court of Elizabeth I from 1595 and who was well known for his athletic prowess, is said to have laid a bet with three other courtiers to swim from Westminster to London Bridge (a distance of about three miles), but the queen forbade the match.[33] Another of Elizabeth's courtiers, Sir Philip Sidney (died 1586) was characterised by Edmund Spenser after his death as a 'strong' swimmer.[34] A tradition of the same period, recorded by the educationist Henry Peacham in 1622, reports that during the engagements of 1588 between the English fleet and the Spanish Armada, 'Gerrard and Harvey, two gentlemen of our own nation ..in the fight at sea swam in the night-time and pierced with augers or suchlike instruments the sides of the Spanish galleons and returned back safe to the fleet'.[35] Christopher Middleton's English translation of Everard Digby's swimming treatise, published in 1595, was dedicated to a gentleman, Master Simon Smith, reputed to possess 'perfection in this faculty'.[36] An interesting picture of a noble youth's dilemma in the 1590s, moved both to learn to swim and not to do so, emerges from the autobiography of Edward Herbert, later Lord Herbert of Cherbury. Writing this work in the 1640s, Herbert concluded,

It will be fit for a gentleman also to learn to swim unless

he be given to cramps or convulsions. Howbeit, I must con-
fess in my own particular that I cannot swim, for as I was
at one time in danger of drowning by learning to swim, my
mother upon her blessing charged me never to learn swimming, telling me further that she had heard of more drowned
than saved by it, which reason though it did not prevail
with me yet her commandment did.[37]

Herbert's inability to swim did not prevent him fearlessly from taking to the water on a swimming horse. His autobiography includes
both recommendations and instructions for teaching one's horse to
swim,[38] and he rode his own steed into the River Usk to rescue his
servant, Richard Griffiths, who had got into difficulties. On this
occasion both men sat on their swimming animals until they reached
the bank, neither of them actually swimming himself.[39]

There is evidence, too, of the skill among the male population
in general. If Everard Digby's original Latin treatise on swimming
was mainly aimed at scholars and gentlemen, Christopher Middleton's
English translation envisaged a wider audience of potential swimmers
among the English reading public who were 'ignorant in the Latin
tongue'.[40] In London the young swimmers of about 1600 resorted to a
'clear water' north of Bunhill Fields 'called Perilous Pond, because
diverse youths swimming therein have been drowned'.[41] Elsewhere, it
is likely that swimming was practised by undergraduates of both the
universities in the late sixteenth century. Pakington and Sidney
were Oxford men, as Digby and Marlowe were of Cambridge. At the
latter swimming caused such alarm, presumably because of its accidents, that on 8 May 1571 the vice-chancellor, John Whitgift, forbade
any scholar of the university to enter any river, pond or water within the county of Cambridge by day or night for the purpose of swimming or bathing, upon pain of the most severe penalties. First
offenders, if undergraduates, were to be beaten publicly and sharply
in the halls of their colleges and again in the university schools
(or lecture rooms). If bachelors of arts, they were to be set in the
stocks for a whole day in their college halls and fined ten shillings.
Second offenders of either grade were to lose their places and be
expelled from the university. Masters of arts and other superior

graduates were to be punished at the discretion of their colleges.[42]
The decree of 1571 accords with other measures taken against dangerous sports at Cambridge. There was an ordinance in 1574 against
scholars going to play games on the Gog-Magog hills,[43] and another in
about 1606 against shooting with guns and the keeping of grey-
hounds.[44] The penalties against swimming of 1571 were more draconian,
but the decree was never republished and its effects may have been
shortlived. When Digby published his treatise in 1587, while still a
member of the university, he gave as one of his reasons for doing so
the number of youths of good family who still came to grief every
year in the Cambridge waters.[45]

Swimming in the sixteenth century recovered some of the status which
it had lost after the Norman Conquest. It was still much regarded
by writers, in the medieval tradition, as a skill for war, but it was
also coming to be viewed as a valuable accomplishment for danger,
health and even recreation. The attitudes of people towards it
varied, as they had also done in medieval times, from the utilitarian
approval of the educationists through the erotic portrayal by Marlowe
to the pessimism of Shakespeare and the downright hostility of Whitgift. Despite the increase of references to it, swimming seems to
have remained a minority accomplishment even among males. It was not
nearly so essential in the *curriculum vitae* of a hero, real or fict-
ional, as the ability to fight well, ride, shoot, speak correctly or
possess good manners. Nevertheless, it rose sufficiently into the
consciousness of scholars to stimulate the writing of specialised
books about it, extolling its virtues and describing its techniques.
To these books we shall turn next.

References

1. *Biblia: The Bible... faithfully and truly translated out of
Douche and Latyn in to Englische*, 1535, Isaiah, fol. 9^v.
2. *The Byble in Englyshe*, London, 1539, part 3, fol. 49.

3. *The Holy Bible*, London, 1611, Isaiah, chapter 25.

4. Cornelius a Lapide, *Commentarii in Scripturam Sacram*, vii, 284-5.

5. Ibid.

6. John Calvin, *Commentarii in Isaiam Prophetam*, Geneva, 1551, p 242.

7. *The Pylgrymage of Sir Richard Guylforde to the Holy Land*, *A.D. 1506*, ed. Sir H. Ellis, London, Camden Society, li (1851), p 76.

8. Francis Fletcher, *The World Encompassed by Sir Francis Drake*, ed. W.S.W. Vaux, London, Hakluyt Society, 1st series, xvi (1854), p 136.

9. Sir Walter Ralegh, *The Discovery of... Guiana*, ed. R.H. Schomburgk, London, Hakluyt Society, 1st series, iii (1848), p 49.

10. Matthew Paris, *Chronica Majora*, ed. H.R. Luard, vol. iv, London, Rolls Series, 1877, p 77.

11. *Mandeville's Travels*, ed. M.C. Seymour, Oxford, 1967, p 215.

12. On this subject see below, chapter 5.

13. On the interest in swimming by 15th-century Italian writers, see W.H. Woodward, *Vittorino da Feltro*, Cambridge, 1905, passim; his *Studies in Education during the Age of the Renaissance, 1400-1600*, Cambridge, 1906, p 37; and P.C. McIntosh, *Landmarks in the History of Physical Education*, 3rd ed., London, 1981, pp 68-70. Dr J.J.G. Alexander has also drawn my attention to Roberto Valturio, *De Re Militari* (composed 1446-55), with an illustration recommending military swimming on boards.

14. Sir Thomas More, *Utopia*, book ii, chapter 8.

15. William Horman, *Vulgaria*, London, 1519, p 278; ed. M.R. James, Roxburghe Club, 1926, pp 401-2.

16. Plautus, *Aulularia*, iv, 9-10.

17. Horace, *Satires*, book i, no. 4, line 120.

18. *The Fovre Bookes of Flauius Vegetius Renatus*, trans. John Sadler, London, 1572, book i, chapter 10.

19. Michael West, 'Spenser, Everard Digby and the Renaissance Art of Swimming', *Renaissance Quarterly*, xxvi (1973), pp 11-22, argues that Sadler by translating 'equites ipsosque equos' merely as 'horses' meant to exclude mounted knights or horsemen from the duty

to swim. This was not in the English tradition of translating Vegetius, however, and *The Oxford English Dictionary* under 'Horse',
section 3 (a, b), quotes 16th-century examples of 'horse' meaning
both the animals and their riders.

20. Sir Thomas Hoby, *The Book of the Courtyer*, London, 1561, fol.
D4; ed. L.E. Opdycke, London, Everyman, 1901, p 42.

21. Roger Ascham, *The Scholemaster*, London, 1570, p 19; *English
Works*, ed. W.A. Wright, 1904, p 217.

22. Sir Thomas Elyot, *The Boke Named the Gouernour*, London, 1531,
fols. 64^V-68; ed. S.E. Lehmberg, London, Everyman, 2nd ed., 1962,
pp 61-4.

23. Sir Thomas Elyot, *The Image of Governance*, London, 1540-1,
fol. 52 (recte 50)^V; *The Scriptores Historiae Augustae*, ed. D. Magie,
vol. ii, London, 1953, pp 236-7.

24. Richard Mulcaster, *Positions*, London, 1581, pp 93-5; ed. R.H.
Quick, London, 1887, pp 94-6.

25. *Renaissance Quarterly*, xxvi (1973), pp 11-22.

26. Spenser, *The Faerie Queene*, book ii, canto vi, verses 42-7.

27. Ibid., book vi, canto iii, verse 34.

28. Ibid., book v, canto ii, verses 7-18.

29. On the dating of the play, see Christopher Marlowe, *Dido
Queen of Carthage and The Massacre at Paris*, ed. H.J. Oliver, London,
1968, pp xxv-xxx.

30. On the authorship of the play, see John Fletcher and William
Shakespeare, *The Two Noble Kinsmen*, ed. G.R. Proudfoot, London, 1970,
pp xiii-xix.

31. The original source is William Malim's preface to Sir Thomas
Chaloner, *De Republica Anglorum Instaurata*, London, 1579, fol. **4-^{V},
reproduced in R. Hakluyt, *The Principal Navigations... of the English Nation*, 2nd ed., 3 vols., London, 1598-1600, ii, 99.

32. The picture is described in detail by Frances A. Yates, 'The
Allegorical Portraits of Sir John Luttrell', *Essays in the History
of Art Presented to Rudolf Wittkower*, ed. D. Fraser, London, 1967,
pp 149-60. The late Dame Frances Yates, unfortunately, did not consider the possibility that the portrait represented stylised human
swimming.

33. *The Dictionary of National Biography*, sub Pakington.

34. Spenser, *Astrophel*, line 74.

35. Henry Peacham, *The Compleat Gentleman*, London, 1622, pp 180-1; ed. V.B. Heltzel, Ithaca, New York, 1962, pp 139-40.

36. C Middleton, *A Short Introduction for to Learne to Swimme*, London, 1595, fol. A2.

37. *The Life of Edward, First Lord Herbert of Cherbury*, ed. J.M. Shuttleworth, London, 1976, p 35.

38. Ibid.

39. Ibid., p 67.

40. Middleton, *A Short Introduction*, fol. A2^V.

41. John Stow, *A Survey of London*, ed. C.L. Kingsford, 2 vols., Oxford, 1908, i, 16.

42. *Statuta Academiae Cantabrigiensis*, Cambridge, 1785, pp 453-4.

43. Ibid., pp 457-8.

44. Ibid., pp 474-5.

45. Everard Digby, *De Arte Natandi*, London, 1587, fol. A4-^{V}.

Chapter Four

EVERARD DIGBY AND HIS 'ART OF SWIMMING'

THE EUROPEAN CONTEXT

The credit for writing the first swimming treatise, like so many
innovations in the history of technology, can be claimed by more than
one person. If we mean by 'treatise' the first published work de-
voted entirely to swimming, the priority must be awarded to Nicholas
Wynman, public professor of languages in the University of Ingolstadt
in Bavaria in 1538. To judge from remarks in his writings, Wynman
was born in Switzerland, which he calls 'our country', and adhered to
the Catholic Church of which his university was a bastion. Three of
his writings survive in print, all Latin works of a light literary
kind: *The Battle of Hercules with Antaeus* (1537), 'an allegorical and
pious interpretation' of the classical fable; *Colymbetes* (1538) on
the art of swimming; and *Dialogues... of Bratislava* (1544). *Colymbetes*, derived from the Greek word for a swimmer or diver, is a
dialogue on swimming, ninety-four pages long, between two characters,
Pampirus and Erotes, the first of them representing the author himself.[1] Through Pampirus, Wynman recalls that he learnt swimming at
the age of thirteen when his mother took him to bathe in the hot
springs close to Sion in the Valais. He was small in stature and she
hoped that the water would relax and increase the size of his body,
because size was important in Switzerland. 'When I saw that boys
were swimming everywhere in the water', he says, 'I longed to imi-
tate them and to learn the art thoroughly.' His first attempts to
swim nearly led to him being drowned, but he persisted more cautious-
ly when other people were present, and in the end he succeeded. The
information in his book was thus a reflection of personal experience.[2]

In his dialogue, Wynman explains how one ought to swim, both on
the front and on the back. He indicates the posture of the body and
the movements of the limbs. He considers the advantages and disad-

vantages of swimming in ponds, rivers and the sea, mentions diving
and considers the possibility of swimming in armour. He seeks to
improve the status of swimming by pointing to some of its famous
exponents from Rome: Horatius Cocles and 'Scaeva', the centurion
identified in the sixteenth century with Plutarch's soldier in Britain. He concludes by reminding the Germans of their own ancient
prowess in the water, described by Herodotus, Caesar and Tacitus.[3]
Wynman thus covers a good deal of ground, but his work remains a
literary essay in praise of swimming—'a merry dialogue and pleasant
reading', as the title-page describes it—rather than a treatise
analysing the skill scientifically. It is not divided into chapters,
it contains no diagrams and its tendency is to stimulate an interest
in swimming rather than to satisfy one. It does not seem to have
made much impact on the public. The work eventually attracted some
interest in the Netherlands, where it was reprinted three times between 1623 and 1644 in a collection of short Latin tracts,[4] but it
was not republished in Germany until the nineteenth century and it
was not translated into French. The author of the first French swimming treatise, Melchisedech Thevenot in 1696, knew only the Dutch
editions, since he calls the author a Hollander,[5] and Wynman is not
mentioned north of the Channel until the translation of Thevenot's
work into English in 1699.[6]

   The subject of swimming was briefly noticed elsewhere in Europe
during the sixteenth century. In Spain, Pedro Mejia (or Mexia)
touched on its nature and value in a short chapter of his *Silua de
Varia Lection* (1550-1), a copy of which belonged to King Edward VI
a year or two later.[7] In Italy a similar short account occurs in
La Piazza Universale by Tommaso Garzoni, published in 1585,[8] and
there may have been others. The achievements of the continental
writers, however, all pale beside the first swimming treatise by a
Briton: Everard Digby's *De Arte Natandi* of 1587. Placed in the context of Europe, Digby's importance is almost as great as it is in
that of Britain. First, he may be rated equal with Wynman for his
originality in conceiving a book about swimming alone. True, Wynman was already in print, but in view of the uncertainty that his
work was known in Britain and the slightness of the accounts by

authors such as Mejia and Garzoni, there is no need to question
Digby's assertion that he was writing the first swimming treatise.
He probably thought that he was, and deserves an appropriate credit.
Second, he undoubtedly surpassed all other writers, including Wynman,
in the scale on which he wrote. Digby produced not simply a literary
discussion but a scientific treatise, the first on the subject. He
identified a wider range of swimming activities and described them
more methodically than anyone else had done. Third, he achieved an
influence which spanned both England and France, and lasted until the
end of the eighteenth century. The history of swimming forms only
one small rivulet beside the great river of European history in general, but Digby is its greatest fish in the sixteenth century and
one of the greatest before the nineteenth.

THE LIFE OF EVERARD DIGBY

The family history of the first British writer on swimming is a difficult matter to penetrate. The Digbys of the sixteenth century were
important and well-recorded people, but there were a great many of
them. Everard Digby, esquire, of Stoke Dry in Rutland, who died in
1509, had seven sons, six of whom founded dynasties, and the name
Everard was given to several of their descendants.[9] Only two of the
sons need concern us: Sir Everard, the eldest, and Rowland, the fifth.
Sir Everard (died 1540) inherited Stoke Dry, and left a son Kenelm
(died 1590) and a grandson Everard (died 1592). The first historians
to deal with the writer on swimming identified him with the latter
Everard,[10] but as Thomas Baker pointed out as early as 1735 this
theory is impossible.[11] Everard Digby of Stoke Dry was a landed
esquire with a child at a time when the writer on swimming was a
fellow of St John's College, Cambridge, and hence a bachelor. A
better candidate can be found among the descendants of Rowland Digby,
who married the heiress of the manor of Welby in Leicestershire.
Rowland's son John inherited Welby and died not long after making
his will on 3 February 1556.[12] In it he mentioned his son and heir
William, his son John and eight other children: Mary, Humphrey,

Kenelm, Everard, George, Eleanor, Margaret and another. These eight
were evidently young, and consequently the children of John's second
wife Jane, daughter of Thomas Ramsey. Their father bequeathed them
two-thirds of his chattels, to be divided equally among them, and
asked Kenelm Digby of Stoke Dry, his first cousin, 'to bring up, set
forth, help and prefer my children until they be married or do come
to their full age'. If we assume the youngest child to have been
recently born in 1555, the likelihood is that Everard's birth took
place in about 1548. These circumstances fit the career of the
writer on swimming. The latter matriculated at Cambridge on 25 October 1567, the right sort of date, as a 'sizar' or poor scholar of
St John's College.[13] In adult life he described his county of origin
as Rutland.[14] This is easily explained if Digby was indeed a poorly
endowed younger son, brought up in Rutland by Kenelm Digby, a pros-
perous esquire who could find him a place at a Cambridge college but
not afford to support him there, hence the sizarship.

As a sizar of St John's, Digby received free or largely free
board, lodging and education in return for acting as a servant to the
fellows of the college and the wealthy students or 'pensioners'.
Sizarships were sought-after offices, and accounted for about half
the admissions to the college at this time. The works of scholarship
which Digby later wrote, characterised by a wide knowledge of Latin
authors and an ambitious but convoluted Latin style, suggest that he
was a clever and diligent student. His progress through the university degree courses and the college hierarchy was certainly a steady
one. In 1570 he was admitted to a college scholarship on the found-
ation of John Keyton,[15] in 1571 he took his BA,[16] in 1573 he was
promoted to a fellowship[17] and in 1574 he graduated as MA.[18] The
fellows of the college were required by statute to take holy orders
and to study theology, so that anyone who wished to hold a fellowship for long had to commit himself to a career as a cleric.[19] Digby
dult made this commitment; as a relatively poor man with no other
career prospects he can have had little alternative. He was ordained
deacon in Peterborough diocese in 1576,[20] and probably priest soon
afterwards, though the record of this is not known. In 1581 he was
admitted to the degree of BD.[21] Meanwhile, he had become involved in

the first of the public disputes which were to make him well known
and indeed notorious to his contemporaries: the Ramist controversy.

In 1579 Digby published his first and chief work of scholarship:
Theoria Analytica in Latin, a demonstration of 'the way to the
mastery... of all philosophy and the rest of the sciences'.[22] The
work consists of a survey of knowledge, an identification of its
branches and proposals for how to study them, based on a wide range
of ancient philosophers particularly Aristotle, but also on certain
continental scholars of the sixteenth century: Scheyk, Carpentarius
and Grouchius. During the course of this book Digby had occasion to
attack the scientific methodology of Peter Ramus (Pierre de la Ramée)
the French Protestant logician, who had proposed a single method for
all purposes of research and teaching: first the definition or com-
prehensive summary, then the explanation of the different parts of
the matter and finally the giving of examples.[23] Digby's attack on
Ramus was controversial, since Ramus's logic was being taught at
Cambridge and he was widely revered by Protestants for having been
killed in the Massacre of St Bartholomew in 1578. A counter-attack
by William Temple, fellow of King's College, was soon published in
1580 with a Latin title which may be translated as *An Admonition to
Everard Digby*, 'seeking the preservation of the single method of
Peter Ramus and the rejection of other methods', the author disguis-
ing his identity under the pseudonym of Francis Mildapet.[24] Temple's
work provoked Digby to a Latin refutation: *A Reply to the Admonition
of F. Mildapet* (1580)[25] and to an amplification of his views about
Ramus, also in Latin, *Two Books on the Double Method*, 'in refutation
of the single method of Peter Ramus, elucidating from the best
authors a plain, easy and exact way towards the understanding of the
sciences' (also 1580).[26] The latter was dedicated to the future Lord
Chancellor, Sir Christopher Hatton, but with what effect is not known.
Finally, Temple responded with a second Latin work, this time under
his own name, *A Dissertation of William Temple* 'on behalf of a de-
fence of Mildapet' (1581), with which the controversy ended.[27] It
does not seem to have been of great moment or influence in the history of English philosophy or scientific thought. Digby emerges as
a well-read man but a conservative exponent of scientific method in

the Aristotelian and scholastic tradition. Temple indeed accused him
of leaning towards the school of Thomas Aquinas, wishing to revive the
sophistries of Duns Scotus and of quoting from the works of other
French and Italian friars of the later middle ages. This is the
first we hear of an innuendo which was to be levelled at Digby later
on: that he was a religious as well as an intellectual conservative,
and a sympathiser with more of Catholicism than its medieval scholarship.

For Digby, however, the early 1580s after the end of the Ramist
controversy were years of prosperity and success. The college statutes permitted fellows to hold a benefice in the Church along with
their fellowships,[28] and Digby now began spending a good deal of time
in attempting to get one. He got his first benefice, the rectory of
Lyndon in Rutland, in 1581 only to give it up by the spring of 1582,
either because he was unable to keep it or did not feel it wealthy
enough for his needs.[29] In January 1582 he petitioned unsuccess-
fully for the rectory of Tinwell, Rutland, in the gift of Lord Burghley,[30] and in August of the same year he acquired the rectory of
Glaston, also in the county, a moderately valuable benefice which he
kept for the rest of his life.[31] In 1583 he gained possession of a
second rectory, Hamstall Ridware in Staffordshire, but this was not
strictly compatible with his fellowship and perhaps for that reason
he resigned Hamstall in 1586.[32] Glaston, at any rate, gave him a
useful additional income, and it was later alleged that he spent much
of his time there rather than at the college. He remained sufficiently active at St John's, however, to be chosen principal lecturer
in 1584 with the duty of lecturing on the arts course to the
scholars and BAs,[33] and a year later he was elected one of the eight
senior fellows of the college, with a higher status and a greater
share in the management of affairs.[34] Finally, in 1587 he published
the book with which we are chiefly concerned: the swimming treatise
De Arte Natandi. The dedication to Richard Wortley, esquire, was
written at St John's on 6 May and the book probably came out in the
summer. Five people contributed verses to it in praise of the
author and his project, including three of his junior colleagues:
Robert Booth, Samuel Goodyear and Otwell Hill, showing that Digby

had friends and supporters in St John's, especially among the younger
fellows. Outwardly in the summer of 1587 he was a moderately successful man: a senior fellow of his college, a beneficed clergyman and
the author of four books, yet his fall was close at hand. Six months
later a train of events began which caused him to lose his fellowship, leave Cambridge and grow a disappointed and embittered man,
reduced to the status of a mere country parson.

The incident which led to Digby's downfall was trivial in itself,
but was magnified by acrimonious personal and religious divisions
within the college. The reigning master of St John's, Dr William
Whitaker, was a prominent figure on the Puritan wing of the Church:
a Calvinist in theology and a vehement anti-Catholic. The college
steward, Henry Alvey, was a strong Puritan too, and Whitaker's close
confidant.[35] Digby, as his writings make clear, belonged at the very
least to the conservative wing of the Church and may have had lean-
ings beyond, though this has never been proved. He had already
revealed his preference for the medieval friar philosophers over
Ramus the Protestant, he was later to publish an attack on the damage
caused by the Reformation to the Church of England, and he belonged
to a family whose senior branch, the Digbys of Stoke Dry, were known
to be Catholics. Whitaker and Alvey were bound to see such a man as
a crypto-Papist and Digby evidently had a hearty dislike of them. He
was not a gentle retiring scholar but, as the evidence will show, a
man of robust and choleric disposition. The matter which brought
about his expulsion from the college could not possibly have had
this effect had it not been for the wider personal and religious
issues involved.

The fellows of St John's were bound to pay the steward every
month for the 'commons' or basic food of themselves and the scholars
and sizars to whom they were tutors.[36] Ordinary fellows had to take
their money to the steward, but since about 1583 it had been agreed
that the steward should call for this purpose on the senior fellows
at their chambers. When Alvey became steward he abandoned this
practice, apparently with Whitaker's consent, and by the autumn of
1587 he had ceased to call for the money. Digby's reply was to
stand on his privilege. He refused to make payment except at his

chamber, with the result that by 22 December 1587 he owed the college
8s. 7d. for one month's commons. According to Digby, Alvey did not
approach him personally about the debt, but simply reported him for
non-payment. John Palmer, the president or master's deputy, mentioned the matter to Digby on three occasions, in what Digby later
claimed to have been an informal manner not an official one, upon
which Digby asked Palmer to call the senior fellows to determine the
controversy, as the college statutes laid down. He also offered to
pay the money if the steward would come to his chamber. Palmer did
not convene the seniors, however, and Alvey steadfastly refused to
call. Finally, on 26 January 1588, Whitaker himself warned Digby
formally about his non-payment in the presence of some of the seniors, after which a third party paid the money to the steward on
Digby's behalf. Notwithstanding this action, Whitaker pronounced on
31 January that Digby was no longer a fellow, on the grounds that he
had refused to pay for his commons after three formal admonitions to
do so.

Digby lodged an appeal at once with the visitors of the college:
the chancellor of the university, Lord Burghley, and the archbishop
of Canterbury, John Whitgift. He alleged that Whitaker had deprived
him for no just cause but out of mere 'displeasure and malice towards him'. The visitors took action, and on 14 February appointed
the vice-chancellor and two senior members of the university to call
Whitaker and Digby before them and to hear evidence about the case.
Whitaker, however, having found a pretext for ridding the college of
his enemy, had no intention of losing the initiative. During the
following weeks he busied himself by writing to the earls of Essex,
Leicester and Warwick—powerful and prominent men who were known to
favour the Puritans—requesting their help in the matter. He also
sent a long statement of his position to Lord Burghley on 4 April,
minutely refuting each one of Digby's objections and adding a list
of twenty-two new charges against him, on religious and personal
grounds.[37] The burden of the first group was that Digby was 'vehe-
mently suspected, upon good presumptions, to be of corrupt religion'.
He had preached at St Mary's church in Cambridge in favour of
'voluntary poverty', one of the principles of monasticism. He had

inveighed against Calvinists in academic disputations, as though they
were schismatics. He kept company with known Catholics in Cambridge,
and had encouraged three members of the college into the holding of
Catholic beliefs. He had spoken 'undutifully', presumably unpatriot-
ically, about the war in the Low Countries and about Sir Francis
Drake. The personal charges portrayed him as a coarse and violent
man, guilty of 'open contempt' of the master and the college government. He had gone about fishing in the Backs with a casting-net,
together with some of the scholars, when he should have been present
in chapel. He was accustomed 'to blow a horn often in the college in
the day time and halloo after it'. He had threatened in public to
set Palmer, the president, in the stocks, and had shouted in Latin
that Palmer was a bad logician, beating with his hands on the table
as he did so. He had finally had the impudence to sit in Whitaker's
place at table, while the master was away.

The charges, no doubt, contain elements of truth, much exagger-
ated by their hostile proponent. Digby's later religious utterances
confirm his conservative religious sympathies, and his book on swimming reflects a taste for hearty outdoor activities. If he was fond
of the river, he may have enjoyed the hunting-field as well. Con-
servatives and sportsmen, however, were both very common among the
Elizabethan clergy, Whitaker himself being a notable fisherman,[38]
and he did not succeed in establishing beyond doubt, any more than
the other evidence does, that Digby was either a Catholic or an
ungovernable ruffian. The visitors were not impressed by the
charges. On 6 April Whitgift and Burghley, having received the report of the vice-chancellor and his colleagues, ordered Digby to be
restored to his fellowship. They conceded that he had been 'unad-
vised and peremptory' in his attitude to the place of payment, but
they accepted that the steward had been used to visit the senior
fellows for money and they found an absolute lack of legality in the
measures taken to warn Digby and to deprive him. The three so-called
admonitions had not been delivered properly either in form or in
timing. The punishment of deprivation was improper in any case,
since the college statutes only provided for a fellow in debt to lose
his chamber and have his goods confiscated to the value of the money

he owed. As for the religious charges against him, these deserved to
be investigated and if proven Digby would have to clear himself of
them. In the meantime, however, he was to remain a fellow of the
college.

If the visitors thought that their judgment would settle the
matter they were quite mistaken. During April the three earls,
prompted by Whitaker, wrote letters to Whitgift attacking Digby and
asking the archbishop to suspend his decision. On 30 April Whitgift
wrote an exasperated letter to Burghley about their efforts. He
accused Whitaker and Palmer of lobbying the earls and stirring up
trouble between himself and them. Whitaker, he said, had acted
contrary to the college statutes, the code of charity and the spirit
of divinity of which he was university professor. He had traduced
Digby before he was judicially heard, by alleging faults which if
they were true he ought to have dealt with as master. On the same
day Whitgift informed Leicester, in similar language, that he had
heard Digby's case deliberately and thoroughly. The proceedings
against him were defective, and Whitaker's charges of no moment. The
archbishop complained that he had always favoured Whitaker and had
helped him to get the mastership. Now, in a cause of his own,
'wherein he is thought to seek his private revenge', Whitaker had resorted to uncharitable and indirect practices. We are left in no
doubt that Whitgift, a fair and disinterested party, thought Whitaker
the villain of the piece, and not Digby. Leicester wrote back almost
immediately on 6 May, however, maintaining the attack and asking now
that if Whitaker would not rescind his judgment, he would order Digby
to leave within a quarter of a year, or at least take away his senior
status. Digby, urged Leicester, was 'a lewd fellow which disturbeth
the /college's/ government and hath impoisoned their youth. Your
grace may very well know that this matter should not so far be urged
but for religion sake, which must needs receive a blow if such a fellow remain among them.'

Leicester's efforts were not successful immediately. On 28 May
1588 Digby was restored to his fellowship by the visitors, but he did
not enjoy his place for very long.[39] A letter of 1 June from Whitaker to Burghley shows that the master remained implacable towards

him, and still held hopes of getting the judgment reversed. The
letter, an ingratiating one, apologises if Whitaker has offended
Burghley, attempts to justify the way in which he has acted, dis-
claims motives of malice or revenge and ends by asking Burghley 'to
look into this cause', presumably in order to reopen it.[40] The college accounts, which run from 21 December each year, reveal that
Digby received no allowance in the first quarter of 1588 during the
dispute, but was given a double allowance for the second quarter in
which he was restored, evidently to make good the arrears of the
first quarter. In the third quarter he received a normal, single
allowance, but in the fourth and subsequent quarters none.[41] This
shows that he vacated his fellowship at about Michaelmas 1588. The
result was a compromise, effectively if not intentionally. By re-
storing Digby in May the visitors asserted their power and Digby was
vindicated. By Digby leaving the college in the autumn satisfaction
was given to Whitaker and his powerful backers, whom Whitgift could
hardly afford to ignore completely. It may be that Digby was offered the chance to resign, in order to save his face, but his own view
of the matter, as we shall see, was that he had been banished and he
evidently went grudgingly. Obliged to withdraw from St John's, he
fell back on the only other resource available to him, the rectory
of Glaston and a career as a country clergyman. In the end he did
not do too badly in this respect. Freed of the restrictions imposed
by his fellowship, he recovered his former benefice of Hamstall Ridware in 1590,[42] and in 1593 he was instituted to a third living, the
rectory of Orton Longueville in north Huntingdonshire.[43] For most
of the rest of his life he had a fair and certainly an adequate income, and at Glaston and Orton, his two chief benefices, he was in
his home country where the name of Digby was respected. We do not
know if he resorted to marriage: the other comfort denied to a
fellow and open to a country clergyman, but it seems unlikely.

In 1590 Digby published his final work, this time in English:
Everard Digbie his Dissuasive 'from taking away the livings and
goods of the Church, wherein all men may plainly behold the great
blessings which the Lord hath poured on all those who liberally have
bestowed on His holy temple and the strange punishments that have

befallen them that have done the contrary'.[44]   The significance of the
date is its coincidence with the famous Marprelate controversy.   In
1588-9 several anonymous Puritan tracts by 'Martin Marprelate' had
made a stir by attacking the English bishops, and defenders of the
established Church were now busily counter-attacking in print.   Digby
appears to have been moved to join in, but the *Dissuasive* is a more
personal document and ranges more widely than the controversy, which
it does not indeed mention by name.   The work makes clear the standpoint of its author which had so antagonised Leicester and Whitaker.
Its 224 pages consist of a lamentation on the sufferings of the
Church of England, highly emotional but sorely long-winded.   It be-
wails the ruin of religious buildings, the misappropriation of endow-
ments meant to maintain learning and charity, and the rise of
reformers greedy for the property which still remained in the hands
of the bishops and cathedral chapters.   Digby was careful to keep
within the bounds of propriety by making complimentary references to
the ruling dynasty.   He admitted that the dispossessed monks and
friars had 'abused' their property, and used much circumlocution in
talking of those who had taken control of monastic lands.   His views,
indeed, although conservative were not incompatible with membership
of the Church of England, many of whose members shared his distaste
at the seizure of Church property for lay purposes and feared lest
the process should go further.   Shakespeare and Donne, only to name
two well-known writers, were to imply their equal sorrow at the dis-
poliation of the Church, in subsequent years.[45]

The biographical value of the *Dissuasive*, apart from confirming
its author's place on the right wing of the Church, lies in its
revelation of Digby's bitterness and disillusionment after the fellowship debacle.   Evidently away from Cambridge, he compares himself
with 'the exiled poet in the sorrowful distress of his banishment'.[46]
He had resolved with himself, he says, never to publish anything else
in print, had it not been for the rise of so much 'sacrilegious zeal'
—presumably the Marprelate tracts.[47]   Wounded by the ending of his
academic career, he returns again and again to the small account
'made of poor scholars at this day', the fruitlessness of their
labours, 'the small comfort which poor scholars have commonly when

they come abroad' and the 'poor contemned scholar' writing of the
princes and orators of the past.[48]   The book exudes the bitterness of
a disappointed man, who took no comfort from his academic publications or his original treatise on swimming. He lived after this for
a few years longer, until the beginning of James I's reign. In 1601
he resigned his living of Hamstall in favour of a relative, another
Everard Digby,[49] and his final years appear to have been spent at
Orton Longueville where he is mentioned as dwelling in 1603 and
where his signature appears regularly in the parish registers.[50]   No
doubt he preferred Orton to Glaston since, lying only two miles from
Peterborough, it was closer to the comforts of town life. On 28
November 1605 the court of the archdeacon of Huntingdon arranged for
the administration of the goods of Everard Digby, formerly rector of
Orton, who had died intestate,[51] and his two benefices were filled by
new rectors shortly afterwards.[52]   This shows that he died in his
late fifties in the autumn of 1605, perhaps at Orton, but there is
no local record of his death or burial.[53]   Oddly enough, he died at
about the time of the Gunpowder Plot in which another of his kinsmen,
Sir Everard Digby of Stoke Dry, was a main participant.

DIGBY'S 'ART OF SWIMMING'

Digby's biography does much to explain why it was he who wrote the
first British treatise on swimming, and why it acquired the form that
it took. For such a work to be written it needed a man of hearty
outdoor tastes, which Digby possessed, in a sufficient milieu of
swimmers, which Cambridge (along with London and Oxford) best provided at that time. It required a scholar, and one with a streak of
eccentricity, to conceive of the possibility of writing such a
treatise and to make the concept real. In the preface to his work,
Digby announced his objective as raising the art of swimming 'from
the depths of ignorance and the dust of oblivion'. He had been
doubtful, he says, whether it was right for him to treat of an activity usually considered boyish, in view of his age and gown (he was
nearly forty at the time). But he had then considered the value of

swimming in times of danger, when other possessions—wealth, friends,
birth and title—were useless. The truth of this had been shown for
many years by youths of good birth being drowned in the waters of
Cambridge. The treatise with which he aimed to prevent such accidents is, like Wynman's, a short work of 115 pages, forty of which
are plates. Like Wynman's too it takes the form of a dialogue between Geronicus the expert and Neugenes the learner, but this conven-
tion was so common in the sixteenth century (and had already been
used by Digby himself) that no significance attaches to the fact.
It was written in Latin not English, and probably for two reasons.
First, Digby wanted to give his subject status and dignity, and
second, he believed that he was writing the first and fundamental
account of it. Swimming, he declares, is an art like medicine, war,
agriculture or navigation. The other arts all have their standard
authors: Virgil on agriculture, Vegetius on war, Hippocrates and
Galen on medicine and Mercator and Ortellius on geography. Swimming,
in contrast, has had 'few, or rather no authors' to describe its
method, which Digby aimed to rectify. He seems to have seen himself,
humorously at least, as the equal of the other definitive writers,
and since they had written in Latin or Greek so would he. By doing
so, however, he limited his potential readership in England to the
aristocracy, clergy and scholars who could read Latin, and made it
difficult for his writings to circulate among the population in general. The original Latin edition was never reprinted, and it took a
series of translations into English gradually to establish the influence of the work during the seventeenth and eighteenth centuries.[54]

The treatise is divided into two books of which, roughly speaking, the first expounds the theory of swimming while the second
explains the techniques. The first book starts by seeking to establish the status of swimming. It is an art: not one of the liberal
arts which are studied by scholars, but a mechanical art like
medicine and chemistry which is concerned with physical matters
(chapters 1-2). These arts in dignity stand next below the liberal
arts, like a handmaiden to a mistress or the body to the mind. The
purpose of swimming, like medicine, is to prolong life, in this case
from the danger of water. Like medicine, too, it promotes health,

purging the skin from uncleanness and moderating the heat of the body
in summer. Some people also practise it for pure amusement. Formally, Digby considered that the most important of these objects was
the first, the saving of life in the water. Like Elyot he was still
sufficiently in the tradition of Vegetius to wish to emphasise swimming as a practical skill. At the same time he shares Elyot's and
Mulcaster's new interest in swimming for health, and in practice his
book considers both this and recreation. He resembles these authors,
too, in assuming that his audience is sceptical of the value of
swimming and needs to be reassured of its safety and propriety. He
therefore goes on to discuss whether swimming is natural.(6-8).
Here he makes the bold assertion that not only is it natural for man
to swim but he excels all beasts in his ability to do so. In this
respect his view of swimming harmonises with the Elizabethan concept
of creation as a great chain or ladder of ranks from God through the
angels and man to the animals, from the most highly developed to the
lowest and inert.[55] The higher the animal stands in the chain of
creation, the better the swimmer. The lion, king of beasts and beast
of the sun, swims well and strongly, while the toad, earthbound in
complexion and heavy by nature, sinks in water. There are certain
exceptions to this rule, since the cock, the bird of the sun, swims
less well than the duck, the bird of Saturn, due to defects of form.
Man surpasses the animals in this as in everything else. Digby as-
sures his readers that the natural tendency of a man in the water is
for his feet to sink but for his face to rise. It is possible for a
man to remain afloat without using his hands or feet, which Digby
promises to explain. Those who perish in the water do so not through
nature but because they use their limbs in a disorderly way. Men
are even superior swimmers to fish. True, fish spend all their lives
in water and do so without breathing, but man can survive in their
element which they cannot do in his. He can also descend perpendicularly, seek and take hold of objects, swim on his back and his
side, stand, sit or throw things in the water, to a far greater extent than any fish.

The first book ends with advice on the time and place for swimming. Here some of the observations seem whimsical today, based as

they are on discarded beliefs about health and the weather, but the
motive for making them was a practical one. Elizabethan swimming,
being done in natural waters such as pools and rivers, encountered
special hazards which Digby recognised and tried to deal with sens-
ibly. The right time of the year for swimming is from May to August (9). Days when the wind is cold should be avoided; the best
winds are from the south and west, the worst from the east and
north (12-13). Swimming at night and in the rain are also ruled out;
the night is unhealthy while rain hurts the eyes and reduces the
visibility, both above and below the water-surface (11, 14). Digby
then offers his readers advice about where they should swim. Places
with overgrown banks are bad, since noisome animals may be found
there, such as snakes and toads, and thorns to hurt the feet. Banks
should be chosen where the grass is short and where there are trees
to offer shade and shelter. The place should possess clear water,
unsullied by grass, straws or filth (16). Muddy places should be
shunned, where sheep are washed or where there is scum on the water.
Great care should be taken lest the bed of the river or pool is deep
or shelves abruptly. The best place is where the bottom is sandy or
rocky. The swimmer is advised to go with a companion who can help
him when necessary. However, if he is alone, he should take a fishing rod with a weight on the end of it, and plumb the depth of the
water before he enters. Finally, he should not go into the water
sweating (17). The body should be brought into a moderate state before entering, neither too hot nor cold.

With these preliminaries over, Digby proceeds in his second book
to explain the techniques of swimming itself. Here his interests in
logic and method make his work a more systematic treatise, to its
credit, than the discourse of Wynman, the teacher of literature. The
second book is divided into forty chapters, each describing one kind
of stroke, feat or manoeuvre for a swimmer to do. The explanations
thus mark an improvement on Wynman's in being separate and categor-
ised, and also in being provided with forty-three woodcuts to illus-
trate the text. The woodcuts are ingeniously devised in two parts: a
frame, showing the banks of a river, into which a small moveable
panel is inserted displaying the swimmer in an appropriate posture.

Variety was achieved by providing five different frames to hold the
panels. Three of them show a river flowing down the picture vertical-
ly, and two across it horizontally. The river banks are grassy and
furnished with trees, as Digby recommended; the sun is out in one of
the frames, and various landscape features are shown: a thatched
house, a windmill, a stile and a herd of cattle. Stakes in the river
remind us of one of the hazards which swimmers encountered. Three
of the frames show figures on the bank as well as in the water: an
Elizabethan gentleman sitting down in hat, ruff, shirt and breeches,
drawing off his stockings, and a naked man running towards the bank
in order to dive. These figures either stand for the novice swimmer
and his companion, or for a single swimmer in two stages of undress.
By modern standards there is something to be desired in the placing
of the illustrations in relation to the text. Only ten are arranged
on the opposite page to the corresponding instructions; the other
thirty-three appear overleaf, and are not well placed for consulta-
tion. The fault, however, may well be that of the printer, not the
author.

   The account of techniques covers most of the subjects proper to
a modern swimming treatise: entry into the water, the basic propulsive strokes, turning, floating, treading water, diving, underwater
swimming and decorative feats. The arrangement begins logically with
the entry (chapter 1). Digby reprehends those who jump into the
water feet downwards, no doubt because he has already pointed out the
danger of getting the legs stuck in a muddy bottom. For the novice,
he recommends entry by wading in gradually, and for the more advanced
swimmer by jumping in so as to present the back or side to the surface and avoid plunging too deep. Having discussed the entry, Digby
explains what he calls 'swimming on the front' (the equivalent of the
modern breast-stroke) (2), how to turn onto the back by rolling the
body (3), and how to do a back-stroke of the Old English variety with
the legs alone (4). After this he describes two methods of changing
direction while swimming: turning while lying on the side (5), and
turning by sweeping the feet underneath in an arc like the swing of a
bell (6). At about this point Digby encountered the problem of all
writers: how to arrange in consecutive order a large number of topics

with no obvious relationship to one another. He evidently changed
his mind at a late stage before publication, since chapters 16-19 of
the second book were brought forward and inserted between chapters
7 and 8 without the numbers being altered. The result, even so, is
not particularly logical, the sequence proceeding through various
back-strokes and rolls (16-19), other kinds of turns (8-9), swimming
on the front with hands together (10), the side-stroke (11) and the
dog-paddle (14). Later chapters describe vertical floating (22),
treading water (23) and a large number of feats with which to amuse
oneself or impress other people. These include sitting in the
water (27), paring one's toe-nails in the water (28), showing four
parts of the body above the water at once (29), carrying articles
above the water (the illustration shows birds being held in the
hands) (31), raising a leg and pretending to put on a boot (32), and
floating on the back while dancing with both legs (33). Of the
latter Digby remarks, 'this is the most difficult of all, and by far
the most remarkable. If you are skilful in this, you have reached
the top; do not contend higher.' The final chapters of the book return to a logical order. They deal with diving: a standing dive
from the bank (34) and how to descend beneath the water (35), underwater swimming on the belly (36), rising to the surface (37), seeking objects on the bottom (38), and 'swimming like a dolphin'—in
other words coming up for air before diving again (39). The fortieth
chapter is a short conclusion.

Whatever the faults of Digby's arrangement, his work attains a
high standard for so original an undertaking. It covers a wide
range of activities. The author provides his readers with the means
to learn how to propel, manoeuvre and enjoy themselves in the water.
His awareness of possible dangers, already mentioned, finds further
expression in his inclusion of two strokes specially useful if one
suffered cramp (12-13) and a third in which the swimmer lies prone
with arms and legs stretched out but close together, for negotiating
water weeds (26). It is bound to be asked whether Digby's descriptions represent idiosyncratic practices of his own or the general
swimming methods of his day. The latter is the more likely. Digby
makes no claims of uniqueness or originality. Nor, except for

criticising one or two dangerous practices (like jumping into the
water feet first) does he propose changes or reforms to what is done.
He does, on the other hand, make references to other people doing
what he describes. These include the various methods of entry into
the water (1), the use of floats by learners (2), and the tendency of
some men to start swimming with the dog-paddle (14). His use of the
latter term and that of the 'bell-turn' to describe one of the turning manoeuvres may also represent contemporary practice. When
Christopher Middleton translated the book eight years later, he felt
no need to interpret or to change it, and its interest to translators
a century later confirms that it embodied the main-stream swimming
tradition, rather than an eccentric version of it. The likelihood is
that the book preserves the best English practices of the day, as
done by those who gathered at Cambridge, and probably of a traditional kind. In the lack of any earlier treatise, it gives us our
nearest glimpse of what are likely to have been the swimming techniques of the middle ages.

What picture, then, emerges of the Tudor swimmer and, by infer-
ence, of his medieval predecessors? By modern standards they were
weak in the efficiency and speed of their basic propulsive strokes.
Digby's instructions for the breast-, side- and back-strokes simply
advise the swimmer to strike out with the arms and legs, and give
little attention to the best form of the strokes for maximising
power and minimising resistance. Early swimming in consequence cannot have been very fast; in 1595 Middleton was to assert that the
side-stroke was the swiftest. Digby's contemporaries did not
achieve the precision with which their modern successors, heirs of
the Industrial Revolution, perform a mechanical sequence of swift,
identical, beautiful strokes. The Tudor swimmer did not lack a
sense of the artistic, but his models were the dancer or the acrobat,
hence the stress on the feats to which the work gives so much space.
He was also more of an individualist than most swimmers today.
Digby does not emphasise social swimming. He suggests only one
companion, and his illustrations never show more than three men
together; even these may be meant to represent the same man. Digby
does not describe life-saving or any kind of competitive swimming or

racing. Such activities may well have taken place, but they did not
call for emphasis in a society which took so seriously the hierarchy
of social ranks. It must have been difficult to arrange races at
Cambridge between scholars and gentlemen all of whom had strong in-
clinations to guard and preserve their individual social status.
Nevertheless, the Tudor swimmer had one strength at least which is
lacking in many habitues of modern indoor pools. He was hardy,
adaptable and used to dealing with the obstacles and perils of the
natural environment. He may have been one of a small minority, en-
gaged in a sport regarded by many with distaste for its dangers. Yet
when doing his extrovert feats, perhaps in front of spectators, he
could be as daring and skilful as any sportsman of his time who kept
to the safety of dry land.

References

1. Nicholas Wynman, *Colymbetes, sive De Arte Natandi*, Augsburg,
1538; ed. K. Wassmannsdorff, Heidelberg, 1889.

2. *Colymbetes*, fols. A8, B1-2.

3. Ibid., fols. F6-8.

4. *Argumenta Ludicrorum et Amoenitatum Scriptores Varij*, Leyden,
1623; *Dissertationes Ludicrarum et Amoenitatum Scriptores Varii*,
Leyden, 1638, 1644.

5. M. Thevenot, *L'Art de Nager*, Paris, 1696, preface.

6. M. Thevenot, *The Art of Swimming*, London, 1699, preface.

7. Pedro Mejia, *Silua de Varia Lection*, Valladolid, 1550-1, part i,
chapter 23, fols. 24^V-25^V. The British Library copy of this work
belonged to Edward VI. Selections from the work, *The Foreste*, translated by Thomas Fortescue, were published at London in 1571, but did
not include the swimming chapter.

8. Tommaso Garzoni, *La Piazza Universale*, Venice, 1585, discourse
112.

9. For a genealogy of the Digby family (not wholly correct) see
J. Nichols, *The History and Antiquities of the County of Leicester*,
4 vols., London, 1795-1815, vol. ii, part 1, p 261/3.

10. J. Strype, *The Life and Acts of John Whitgift, DD,* 3 vols., Oxford, 1822, i, 516-21, and C.H. & T. Cooper, *Athenae Cantabrigienses,* vol. ii: *1586-1609,* Cambridge, 1861, pp 146-7, followed by J. & J.A. Venn, *Alumni Cantabrigienses, Part I: ...to 1751,* 4 vols., Cambridge, 1922-7, ii, 41.

11. *Hearne's Collections,* ed. H.E. Salter, vol. xi, Oxford, Oxford Historical Soc., lxxii, 1918, p 462; so also Sidney Lee in *The Dictionary of National Biography,* vol. xv, London, 1888.

12. London, Public Record Office, Probate Court of Canterbury, Prob 11/38 fol. 55-^{v} (PCC 9 Kechyn).

13. J. & J.A. Venn, *Alumni Cantabrigienses,* ii, 41.

14. On his admission as scholar and fellow of St John's, 1570 and 1573 (Cambridge, St John's College, MS Register of Officers, Fellows and Scholars, vol. i, pp 234, 150).

15. 9 November (ibid., p 234).

16. *Grace Book Δ Containing the Records of the University of Cambridge... 1542-1589,* ed. J. Venn, Cambridge, 1910, p 242.

17. 12 March (St John's College, MS Register of Officers, p 150).

18. *Grace Book Δ,* p 271.

19. *Early Statutes of the College of St John the Evangelist, Cambridge,* ed. J.E.B. Mayor, Cambridge, 1859, p 125.

20. J. & J.A. Venn, *Alumni Cantabrigienses,* ii, 41.

21. *Grace Book Δ,* p 342.

22. Everard Digby, *Theoria Analytica,* London, 1579.

23. On Digby and the Ramist controversy, see N.W. Gilbert, *Renaissance Concepts of Method,* New York, 1960, pp 200-9.

24. [William Temple], *Francisci Mildapetti Navarreni ad Everardum Digbeium Anglum, de unica P. Rami methodo,* London, 1580.

25. Everard Digby, *Admonitioni F. Mildapetti Responsio,* London, 1580.

26. Everard Digby, *De Duplici Methodo Libri Duo,* London, 1580.

27. William Temple, *Pro Mildapetti de Unica Methodo,* London, 1581, & Frankfurt, 1583.

28. Statutes of 1580, chapter 28, printed in *Second Report from the Select Committee on the Education of the Lower Orders,* London, House of Commons, 1818, p 441.

29. Digby 'compounded' (bound himself to pay tax) for Lyndon on 18
July 1581 (Public Record Office, Exchequer-First Fruits, Composition
Books, E 334/9 fol. 234). The next known rector of Lyndon, William
Thorowgood, was instituted on 2 March 1583 (H.I. Longden, *Northamp-*
tonshire and Rutland Clergy from 1500, 16 vols., Northampton, 1938-
52, xiii, 213).

30. London, British Library, Lansdowne MS 34, no 12.

31. He compounded for Glaston on 6 August 1582 (E 334/10 fol. 19).

32. Digby was instituted to Hamstall on 14 October 1583 and his
successor on 14 November 1586 (W.N. Noble, *Staffordshire Incumbents*
and Parochial Records, 1530-1680, London, William Salt Archaeological Soc., 1916 for 1915, pp 113-14).

33. 9 July (St John's College, MS Register of Officers, p 105).

34. 10 July (ibid., p 14).

35. On Whitaker and Alvey, see H.C. Porter, *Reformation and Re-*
action in Tudor Cambridge, Cambridge, 1958, passim.

36. The documents concerning Digby's case are nearly all printed
by R.F. Scott, *Notes from the Records of St John's College, Cam-*
bridge, Third Series, 1906-13, reprinted from *Eagle* (the college
journal), xxviii, no. 141, December 1906, pp 1-23.

37. The complete text, in British Library, Lansdowne MS 57, no.
78, is printed by J. Heywood & T. Wright, *Cambridge University*
Transactions during the Puritan Controversies of the 16th and 17th
Centuries, 2 vols., London, 1854, i, 506-21.

38. Izaak Walton, *The Compleat Angler*, London, 1653, part i, chapter 1.

39. Cambridge University Library, University Archives, Registrum
pro Actis Curie Academie Cantebr', 1577 (Buckle), pp 568-9.

40. Heywood & Wright, *Cambridge University Transactions*, pp 532-3.

41. R.F. Scott, *Notes from the Records of St John's*, pp 22-3.

42. Digby was re-instituted on 5 December 1590 and his successor
on 22 July 1601 (above, note 32).

43. W.N. Noble, 'Incumbents of the County of Huntingdon', *Trans-*
actions of the Cambridgeshire & Huntingdonshire Archaeological
Society, iii (1914), p 162.

44. London, no date; the book was authorised by the bishop of

London and registered on 2 March 1590 (E. Arber, *A Transcript of the Registers of the Company of Stationers of London, 1554-1640*, vol. ii, London, 1875, fol. 253^v).

45. Shakespeare, *Sonnets*, no. 73, line 4; Donne, *Holy Sonnets*, no. 18, lines 3-4.

46. *Dissuasive*, p 1.

47. Ibid., introduction.

48. Ibid., introduction (twice), p 62.

49. Above, notes 32, 42.

50. C.W. Foster, *The State of the Church in... the Diocese of Lincoln*, vol. i, Lincoln, Lincoln Record Society, xxiii (1926), pp 211, 285.

51. Huntingdon, County Record Office, Huntingdon Archdeaconry Act Book, no. 1, 1559-1614. I am most grateful to Mr A.D. Hill, Senior Archivist, for this information.

52. Longden, *Northamptonshire and Rutland Clergy*, ii, 97 (Glaston); Public Record Office, E 334/14 fol. 59^v (Orton).

53. The Revd. K.P. Lingham, rector of Glaston, and Mr A.D. Hill have kindly informed me that there is no record of Digby's death in the burial registers of Glaston, Orton Longueville, Orton Waterville or Botolph Bridge.

54. There are copies of the *De Arte Natandi* today in the British Library, London (2); Bodleian Library, Oxford; Emmanuel College, Cambridge; Bibliothèque Nationale, Paris; and Boston Public Library, Boston, Mass.

55. The idea is discussed by E.M.W. Tillyard, *The Elizabethan World Picture*, London, 1943.

Chapter Five

DIGBY'S SUCCESSORS AND THE SEVENTEENTH CENTURY

CHRISTOPHER MIDDLETON

It remains now to consider the impact and influence of the *De Arte Natandi* on the subsequent history of swimming in Britain. The first sign of an impact is to be found eight years later with the publication in 1595 of an abridgement of the work in English, entitled *A Short Introduction for to Learne to Swimme*, translated by Christopher Middleton. The translator was a writer of miscellaneous works of prose and poetry, four or five of which were issued under his name in the 1590s, the book on swimming being the earliest. It was followed by *The Historie of Heaven* (1596)—a poem on the stars and the mythology associated with them, *The Famous Historie of Chinon of England* (1597)—a knightly romance in prose, and *The Legend of Humphrey Duke of Glocester* (1600)—an historical poem written, like *The Historie of Heaven*, in stanzas of six lines. A fifth work called *The Nature of a Woman* (1596) by 'C.M.', a prose romance in two parts published separately, is probably also by Middleton. It is similar in character to his other productions and its publisher, Clement Knight, was the printer of *The Historie of Heaven* which appeared in the same year.[1]

The identity of Middleton is an elusive matter on which his works themselves throw little light. The *Short Introduction* was addressed to a 'worshipful and well accomplished gentleman, Master Simon Smith' of uncertain identity, and the next two publications were not even given dedications by the author, these being provided instead by the printers. The best evidence comes from *Humphrey Duke of Glocester* which was dedicated by Middleton to Sir Gervase Clifton, at the suggestion of a gentleman 'your worship's well-willer and my very good friend'. Clifton, an associate of the earl of Essex, was a landowner in Somerset and Huntingdonshire, MP for the latter county in 1597-8 and 1601, and subsequently created Lord Clifton of

Leighton Bromswold in 1608. The dedication to him represents Middleton's one attempt to gain influential patronage for himself by means
of his publications. *Humphrey Duke of Glocester* is also revealing
because it is prefaced with Latin verses in praise of the author by
Robert Allott and English ones by the poets Michael Drayton and John
Weever. That of Drayton calls Middleton his 'friend' and styles him
'Master'. The four men evidently formed a group, since Weever's
Epigrammes, published in 1599, include one addressed to Drayton and
another to Allott and Middleton jointly. Drayton indeed appears to
have had a literary influence on Middleton as well, since *Humphrey
Duke of Glocester* follows the genre of two of his own historical
poems: *The Legend of Piers Gaveston* (1593) and *The Tragicall Legend
of Robert Duke of Normandie* (1596). In general, we gain from Middleton's published works the impression that their author was a modest
man, both in personality and rank. His closest friends were poets
and a scholar, and he did not enjoy the patronage of anyone of great
importance.

Outside his writings, Middleton has been identified with men at
both Oxford and Cambridge in the late sixteenth century. The Oxford
candidate, who matriculated at the age of twenty as a gentleman at
Brasenose College in 1580, is not likely.[2] Middleton is never
styled a gentleman in his publications, and talks of himself as a
young man in the dedication of his swimming treatise, which would
not suit a thirty-five year-old in 1595. There are two reasons, on
the other hand, for seeking to identify him with a man of the same
name at Cambridge who matriculated as a sizar of St John's College
at Easter 1587.[3] First, two of Middleton's friends appear to have
been Cambridge men. Allott is probably identical with another sizar
of St John's who matriculated in about 1592, graduated BA in 1595-6,
MA in 1597 and became a fellow of the college in the same year.[4]
Weever was certainly admitted as a sizar of Queen's College, Cambridge, in 1594 and took his BA in 1597-8.[5] Residence at the same
university may well have brought the three together. Drayton was
not a university man, and is more likely to have met Middleton when
he, Drayton, was working as a playwright in London between 1599 and
1602. Second, there is the circumstance that Middleton's translation

of Digby was his first acknowledged published work when, according to
the dedication, he was a young man. Middleton was not a hack or a
career author; his slender output and lack of interest in dedications
suggest that his works were primarily labours of love. The *Short
Introduction*, as we shall see, reveals a knowledge of swimming independent of its exemplar, and in the preface Middleton is complimentary to Digby in a sense which in 1595 established him as one of
Digby's partisans. He is careful to say that his work is translated
from Digby's book, he praises Digby's 'worth, whose labour first
brought this work within the rules of art' and he endorses Digby's
comparison of himself with Virgil, Vegetius and Hippocrates. This is
explicable if we identify Middleton with the sizar who entered St
John's in the very year that Digby published his treatise and when he
was still in residence there. The rest of Middleton's life is uncertain. He may have died in about 1600, or he may be the same as a
man who took holy orders and became rector of Aston-le-Walls, Northamptonshire, in 1612. This Christopher Middleton received the degree
of BD from both Cambridge and Oxford in 1619 and was buried at Aston
in 1628.[6]

     Middleton's object in writing on swimming was somewhat different
from Digby's. The latter had cast his book as a grand treatise in a
learned style which, Middleton truly observes, 'exceedeth the capacity of the greater part of men'. The *Short Introduction*, as its
title implies, was a simplified version, shorter in length and de-
signed to spread Digby's information to a wider range of people or,
as Middleton puts it, 'to uncurtain that to the view of all which was
only appropriated to a few'. It reproduces accurately the material
of Digby's work but does so more briefly and in the simpler form of a
monologue, not a dialogue. The theory of swimming, which occupies
seventeen chapters (nineteen pages) in Digby's first book, is reduced
to four sections (six and a half pages) in Middleton's, while still
including the most essential topics: the usefulness of swimming,
swimming among the animals, man's ability to swim naturally, and the
times and places proper for doing so. The rest of the *Short Introduction* follows closely the form of Digby's second book, reproducing
all the original thirty-nine chapters in the same order and only

omitting the conclusion. The directions for how to do the strokes
and feats are short and direct, without literary ornamentation. The
text is accompanied by the same illustrations as those of Digby's
work, the blocks of which were evidently acquired by Middleton's
printer, James Roberts. Roberts did not observe great care, however,
with regard to the illustrations. He does not seem to have had a
copy of Digby's work before him, since he inserted the central panels
into their frames without any relation to Digby, so that about two-
thirds of the panels appear in different frames. In two cases
(plates 39 and 40) he managed even to place the panels upside down.

Middleton added very little of his own to Digby's text, but what
he did is interesting. Discussing the hazards which swimmers should
look for in the water, Middleton warns 'that there be not in the bottom of the river any old stakes'. Of what we now call the side-
stroke he observes that 'this kind of swimming, though it be more
laborious, yet is it swifter than any of the rest', thus emphasising
the limitations of the other forward strokes. When describing the
method of changing direction in the water while lying on the side
(Digby's chapter five), he notes that this 'is commonly called the
roach turn' since it resembles 'roach when in the pleasant heat of
summer they wantonly frisk to and fro'. This raises the question of
early swimming terminology, of which the term is a rare example.
Digby, writing in Latin, had invented a terminology by borrowing a
number of sonorous words to denote the techniques he described:
convolutio, retrogradatio, prolapsio and subnatatio. None of these
was adopted by Middleton, however, who only reproduces the one or two
of Digby's terms which seem to have sprung from real Elizabethan
usage. These, as already mentioned, were the 'bell turn' and the
notion of 'swimming like a dog', which anticipates the modern idea of
the dog-paddle. On the whole, Middleton and Digby preferred descriptive phrases to technical terms. They talk of 'swimming upon the
back' or 'on the belly' or 'on the side', not of the 'back-stroke',
'breast-stroke' or 'side-stroke' which did not develop as terms until
the late nineteenth century. Middleton uses the verb 'to strike'
meaning 'to hit the water', but he varies it with 'beat' and 'thrust',
and the noun 'stroke' is unknown to him in the context of swimming.

All this goes to show that Elizabethan swimmers possessed hardly any
generally accepted terms for their skill. Those that existed were
largely informal, and probably varied from person to person.

Middleton's own additions to Digby show that he himself was a
swimmer, or at least a close observer of the skill, and suggest the
probability that he wrote for love, not money. His work, however,
seems to have had but a modest success. No second edition was ever
produced, and although this was also true of Digby's *De Arte Natandi*,
it is likely that Middleton's book had a more limited circulation
still. Only two of its copies survive today, compared with at least
six of Digby's treatise,[7] and whereas the latter was translated into
English twice more in the course of the seventeenth century, there is
almost no evidence that anyone remembered Middleton's version after
1600.[8] Its author, like Digby, was a pioneer well in advance of his
public.

SEVENTEENTH-CENTURY SWIMMING

The history of swimming in the seventeenth century resembles that of
the sixteenth. As before, many traditional ideas and practices concerning the skill remained intact and were transmitted throughout the
century, and as before some changes also took place, especially after
1650, as swimming became influenced by developments in other fields.
Swimming in Stuart Britain continued to be mentioned in educational
writings, in imaginative literature and in one new genre: the literature of science. Two more swimming treatises were published, and
there are documentary records of swimming in practice. As far as
education is concerned, the writers of the early seventeenth century
exhibit little advance upon Elyot's *Governor* in their attitude to the
skill. James Cleland's work *Hero-Paideia*, 'or the institution of a
young noble man' was published in 1607, and *The Compleat Gentleman* by
Henry Peacham in 1622 with three subsequent reprints.[10] Both copy
Elyot closely by listing swimming in a chapter along with other manly
exercises such as riding and running, reproduce his six classical
references to swimming and follow him in depicting it primarily as a

practical skill for preserving oneself in war or other danger.
Neither shows any knowledge of Mulcaster's discussion of swimming for
health or of Digby's treatise, but they agree that swimming was re-
quisite for all noblemen and gentlemen, although Cleland quotes Elyot
almost exactly to the effect that it was 'not much used of noble
men'. A more original writer was Sir George Buck, whose account of
education in London, *The Third Universitie of England*, was published
in 1615. Buck set out to describe all the educational institutions
of the capital, including the facilities for learning athletics, and
gave one paragraph to swimming, albeit a short one. He knew of and
cited the works of Digby and Middleton, and was aware of the European writings on the subject by Mejia and Garzoni. His judgment of
the skill, however, was still in the tradition of Vegetius (whom he
mentions) and Elyot. Swimming 'is needful for all men', but 'it is
most necessary and important to a soldier'.[11] The military motive
still predominates, and there is no interest in swimming for health
or for pleasure.

Not all Stuart educational writers were as traditional as these.
Already in the 1610s more pragmatic views of swimming were being pro-
pounded in which less deference was paid to the exploits of classical
swimmers and more attention given to the practical advantages and
disadvantages of swimming in the contemporary world. Fynes Moryson
in his *Itinerary* of 1617, which if not strictly educational was at
any rate an instructive treatise for travellers, discusses the value
of swimming in practical and non-military terms. Some, he observes,
advise a traveller to learn to swim, and it is true that Caesar saved
himself by doing so, but not all are so fortunate nor are all waters
like that in which he swam. Moryson says that he himself has known
many excellent swimmers, of whom some were drowned at sea in sight
of land, through the fury of the waves or by fearful companions drag-
ging them down, whereas other non-swimmers had reached the shore by
clinging to chests or pieces of wood. His conclusion is that swimming serves 'more for pleasure at home than of use abroad, and yields
small comfort or help in a storm at sea'. If a man wishes to put his
trust in the skill, let him conceal it, 'lest others trusting therein take hold of him and make him perish with them'.[12] These emphases

on care and swimming for pleasure rather than safety are repeated in
Francis Osborn's *Advice to a Son*, published in 1656. Osborn advises
that swimming 'may save a man in case of necessity', but 'it loseth
many when practised in wantonness by increasing their confidence'.
He tells his son that he may swim for pleasure, but should not exceed his depth, and in seeking to save another should beware of
drowning himself.[13] The practical note continues in John Locke's
work, *Some Thoughts concerning Education* (1693), which likewise
fails to make the traditional citations of the classics. Locke
places a high value on boys being made hardy by exercise and expos-
ure to the open air, and accordingly thinks well of swimming in cold
water during the summer as leading to this end. For him the primary
object of swimming is health, and he does not mention pleasure, war
or safety. A boy should learn it when he is old enough and has
someone to teach him, and the only cautions required are constitu-
tional ones: not to go into the war when hot or agitated.[14] Moryson,
Osborn and Locke reveal that educationists, as the seventeenth century progressed, began to break free of the influence of Vegetius and
Elyot. They were more pragmatic in their attitudes to swimming, and
less deferential to the traditions of the past.

    That Locke could see swimming primarily as a healthy pursuit
was possible because, as the century wore on, the subject came in-
creasingly to be dealt with in medical and scientific terms, as well
as those of war and education. We have seen how Mulcaster and Digby
had begun to discuss the advantages and disadvantages of swimming to
health in the 1580s, and this discussion was continued in the 1620s
by Francis Bacon and Robert Burton. Burton in *The Anatomy of Melancholy* (1621, with revisions to 1652) considered whether bathing in
warm or cold water was better for the human body. He mentions
appreciatively the use of artificial warm baths, but 'of cold ones',
he noted, 'I find little or no mention in any physician; some speak
against them. Carden alone [Girolamo Cardano, died 1576] commends
bathing in fresh rivers and cold waters, and adviseth all such as
mean to live long to use it.'[15] Burton appears not to have made up
his mind fully on the subject, but to have been doubtful about the
benefits of cold water, which obviously held implications for

swimming. Bacon, however, argued the contrary opinion in his work,
Historia Vitae et Mortis (1623). To him, warm baths were bad and unhealthy, and the physicians he knew declared they should be avoided.
It was washing in cold water that aided longevity, and fresh-water
baths, only just lukewarm, were highly commendable in summer. Exercise in cold water, such as swimming, was also very good, and 'as a
general rule, exercise in the open air is better than under cover'.[16]
No doubt the views of Bacon and Burton each found their adherents,
attracting some to swimming and bathing while deterring others. Their
younger contemporary, Sir Thomas Browne, is notable because his book
Pseudodoxia Epidemica (1646) displays more fully than theirs the beginnings of an interest in swimming from the standpoint of the new
sceptical and experimental science of the century: that of the 'Scientific Revolution'. In chapter six of this work, Browne sets out to
discuss and disprove three popular fallacies about swimming and floating: 'that men swim naturally if not disturbed by fear; that men being drowned and sunk do float the ninth day when their gall breaketh;
that women drowned swim prone, but men supine or upon their backs'.
With regard to the first he argues (against Digby, but without men-
tioning him) that it does not follow that man swims naturally because
the animals do. Animals swim in the same manner that they go on land,
but man when swimming alters his natural posture by lying prone and
moving his legs in unusual ways. Swimming, in consequence, is an art,
and some people never attain it. There is nevertheless more of nature
in it than in some other habits, because once learnt it is never
discarded, 'nor is there any who from disuse did ever yet forget
it'.[17]

The development of the new science reached an important stage
with the establishment between 1660 and 1682 of the Royal Society,
for the study, discussion and publication of scientific work. The
diary of John Evelyn, who was one of the founding members of the
society, shows that swimming and diving were matters of interest
among them from time to time. He notes in 1663 that the society
considered 'another experiment for diving', in 1667 that Charles
II (the society's patron) 'discoursed with me much about swimming',
and in 1672 that the society received a letter from Greenland 'of

recovering men that had been drowned'.[18] The question of diving attracted the attention of another prominent member of the early society, the Honourable Robert Boyle. In his *New Experiments Physico-
Mechanicall touching the Spring of Air* (1660), he considered in a
critical way the ability of men to breathe under water while diving.
It had long been believed that pearl divers in the Mediterranean and
the tropics could stay under water for very long periods. Bacon had
reported the belief in his *Historia Vitae et Mortis* without examining
it,[19] and Boyle quotes assertions that divers in the West Indies
could remain beneath the surface for an hour and that a Sicilian had
stayed below for three or four times as long. The significance of
Boyle's approach is that instead of adopting these second-hand assertions without question, he followed them with first-hand evidence on
the matter 'from an ingenious man of my acquaintance, who is very
famous for the useful skill of drawing goods, and even ordnance, out
of sunk ships'——in other words a salvage diver. This man, being
asked by Boyle how long he could stay at a depth of fifty or sixty
feet without breathing, confessed that he could not do so for more
than two minutes, and was only able to remain below longer by resort-
ing to artificial aids. One of these, 'a certain engine' of which
Boyle took a description, was perhaps a kind of diving bell, and the
other consisted of small oiled sponges which the diver chewed in his
mouth.[20] The account shows a scientific interest both in how men
survive in the water and in how their survival might be improved. By
the end of the century such interests were to penetrate the swimming
treatises themselves, as we shall see in the case of the one which
came out in 1699.

     At the same time, the interest in swimming did not develop in
practical and scientific directions alone. A romantic idea can also
be traced which, as in the Tudor period, was especially embodied in
imaginative literature. The last years of the seventeenth century
saw the beginnings of a new kind of literary interest in the native
inhabitants of the Third World: the concept of the 'noble savage'.
Primitive peoples, as we have seen, had been known since medieval
times, but the majority of writings about them, both scientific and
imaginative, had tended to dwell on the limitations and sufferings of

of their lives: paganism, cruelty and poverty, rather than emphasising their positive virtues. The reverse began to be the case with
the publication in 1688 of Aphra Behn's novel *Oroonoko: or The Royal
Slave*, the principal work which established the notion of the savage
as the possessor of physical powers and moral virtues which had been
lost by 'civilised' peoples. Mrs Behn's account of the Indians of
South America depicts them morally 'in the first state of innocence,
before men knew how to sin', and physically in a condition of absolute perfection, both in their powers and appearance. They are as
swift as hounds when they hunt and can 'run down the nimblest deer',

> But in the water, one would think they were gods of the
> rivers, or fellow-citizens of the deep; so rare an art
> they have in swimming, diving, and almost living in water,
> by which they command the less swift inhabitants of the
> floods.[21]

Mrs Behn does not describe how the Indians swam, and it was left till
the nineteenth century for native swimming to be studied and copied
by Europeans. The immediate effect of her book and others like it,
however, may have helped to soften prejudice against entering the
water and have assisted the rise of bathing in the eighteenth century. What had before been tainted as an activity of primitive peoples may, perhaps, have become more desirable as these peoples came
to be thought of as models of health and beauty.

The idea of the noble savage, and the portrayal of his prowess
as a swimmer, found further expression in an even more famous and
influential work than *Oroonoko*: Daniel Defoe's *Robinson Crusoe* of
1719. This story contains several mentions of swimming, which Defoe
evidently believed to be a widespread accomplishment among males,
since he ascribes the power to Crusoe himself—an Englishman, to a
north-African Moor and to the Indians of South America.[22] His attitude to the latter was more judicious than that of Mrs Behn, since he
includes among them tribal warriors and cannibals as well as the vir-
tuous civilisable Friday. This diversity is also true of their physical powers. Friday himself, like the natives of *Oroonoko*, is a good
runner, dexterous with a canoe and able to swim well. When he flees
from his enemies by swimming a creek,

> he made nothing of it, though the tide was then up, but
> plunging in, swam through in about thirty strokes or
> thereabouts, landed, and ran on with exceeding strength
> and swiftness.[23]

Of the three savages who follow him, however, one cannot swim at all
and the others do so more slowly than Friday, enabling him to escape.
Natives are not all supermen. Defoe was of the new age in setting
the story among savages, and possibly in making his hero Crusoe wear
breeches, despite his solitude, during his planned swim to the wrecked ship.[24] This differs from the traditional portrayal of swimmers
as naked, and may foreshadow the rise of the use of clothes for bathing during the eighteenth and nineteenth centuries. The author seems
also to reflect a scientific interest in swimming techniques in
describing how Crusoe breathed and positioned himself in the water
after the shipwreck; he was modern, too, in perceiving Friday's swimming as a succession of strokes (as we do), and in estimating their
number.[25] He was still a traditionalist, however, in viewing swimming primarily as a practical skill to save life in time of danger,
and he does not present it in terms either of health or recreation.

In this respect even the imaginative writers do not complete the
picture of swimming as it was, since seventeenth-century records suggest that real swimmers practised the skill for pleasure quite as
much as for self-preservation. Sir William Sanderson, whose acquaintance with the king's court went back to James I, asserted in 1650
that immoderate swimming was one of the athletic pursuits, over-
indulged in, which led to the death of Henry Prince of Wales in 1612.
'He retired to his house at Richmond, pleasantly seated by the Thames
river, which invited him to learn to swim in the evenings after a full
supper.'[26] In 1615 Sir George Buck evidently considered that swimming
was widely in use in London since he observes that 'this art can many
men in this town teach very well'—the earliest clear reference in
England to specialised swimming instructors—and that 'for commodity
of river and water for that purpose there is nowhere better'.[27]
William Prynne's *Divine Tragedie* of 1636, 'a collection of sundry memorable examples of God's judgments upon Sabbath breakers', describes
five fatal accidents of which he had heard arising from swimming on

Sundays. All took place in or near London where Prynne was writing
and appear to be authentic, two of them being precisely dated to 1635.
One case involved a young man from 'near Bow' and another two young
men of the parish of St Dunstan-in-the-West, the former taking place
in the River Thames on the Essex side. At St Albans a boy who went
swimming in Verulam Ponds a mile away was drowned and another scarce-
ly escaped, while at Ramsey in Suffolk,

> a tall man on the Lord's day going with others to swim,
>
> and being advertised and warned of a hole in the water,
>
> he swore that there was no place that could drown him,
>
> but by and by on a sudden he was missing, being now under
>
> water, and so drowned.[28]

John Evelyn certainly entered the water from time to time for bathing,
though he does not mention swimming. In July 1650 he bathed in the
pond by his house at Wotton in Surrey 'after I had not for many years
been in cold water', and in August of the following year he and his
wife watched French ladies bathing in the Seine at Conflans and ended
by bathing themselves, 'it being exceeding hot weather'. In 1654 he
bathed at Bath.[29]   Robert Boyle in 1660 describes

> a corpulent man, who is wont to descend to the bottom of
>
> the Thames, and bring out of deep holes at the bottom of
>
> the banks large fishes alive in his hands,[30]

apparently as a feat to amuse spectators. At Oxford, undergraduates
are mentioned swimming in Merton Pool and 'Schollers Pool' in 1667,
and in 1689 the first allusion is made to 'Patten's /later Parson's/
Pleasure', the bathing place on the River Cherwell which has been
frequented by male nude bathers down to modern times.[31]   The Evelyn
and Oxford references may indicate an increase of fashion in bathing
or swimming in rivers, but the scarcity of early swimming references
in general makes it difficult to be sure.

WILLIAM PERCEY AND MELCHISEDECH THEVENOT

The second half of the seventeenth century saw the publication of two
more swimming treatises in English, both of them largely translations

of Digby's *De Arte Natandi*. The first of these, *The Compleat Swimmer*
(1658), was the work of a certain William Percey, gentleman.[32] Apart
from the mention of his status, the book supplies no evidence about
his identity which remains a mystery. He was enough of a Latinist to
be able to grapple with Digby's elaborate style, but not to avoid a
most egregious blunder concerning Ovid: 'If Hero had been skilled
herein, he had not lost his love-sick life in swimming to his Leander'! The work begins with a preface recalling the author's youth and
his first acquaintance with water:

> I remember when I was a school-boy, delighting much in hot
> weather to bath in our country rivulets, I once was in
> danger of drowning; but by the help of another that could
> swim was saved... which danger wrought in me such an earn-
> est desire to learn to swim that I seldom did forbear the
> exercise a day, till I was become a perfect swimmer.

Percey goes on to extol the value of swimming for pleasure, exercise,
health and the preservation of life, and recommends the skill not
only to males but, significantly, females. 'I could very well wish
every man and woman were perfect in swimming likewise, which with a
little practice they easily may attain unto.' The book itself, on
the other hand, seems to assume as Digby had done that the practitioners will all be men.

The form and content of Percey's treatise is entirely based upon
Digby, of which like Middleton's work it is an abridged translation.
Percey, however, made absolutely no mention of Digby or any acknowledgement of his debt, thus branding himself a plagiarist, which
suggests that Digby's work had largely been forgotten by the mid
seventeenth century. There is no evidence that Percey knew of Middleton or used his book. *The Compleat Swimmer* contains fifty-one
chapters, of which the first eleven summarise the seventeen chapters
of Digby's first book, while the last forty are an abridgement of the
thirty-nine chapters of the second. The work is less useful than
Middleton's because it contains no diagrams, and it probably achieved
little impact; at all events it was never reprinted. It is of interest, nonetheless, in one small respect. Writing of swimming on the
back, Percey observes that it is easy to splash oneself 'at every

stroke', but that with care the problem is avoided.[33] This is one of the earliest literary records of the word 'stroke' to mean a swimmer's action. The term was evidently just beginning to come into vogue, since Percey only uses it twice, and for the rest of the time he resorts to descriptive phrases as his predecessors had done.

Only a little more honest than this was the translation of Digby's treatise into French by Melchisedech Thevenot: *L'Art de Nager*, published at Paris in 1696 and retranslated into English as *The Art of Swimming* three years later. Thevenot, who was born in about 1620, served as an agent of the French crown at Genoa in 1645 and at Rome in 1652-4, after which he settled down to a life of scholarship. Between 1663 and 1689 he published four volumes of voyages by travellers to various parts of the world, revealing that he had an interest in the sea and in native peoples from which a concern with swimming may have arisen. In 1684 he became keeper of the royal library of Louis XIV, and he died at Issy near Paris on 29 October 1692.[34] *L'Art de Nager*, published four years later, was consequently issued posthumously. In his preface Thevenot claimed that his treatise was the first to appear in French and that he only knew of two authors who had written on the subject before him: Everard Digby, 'of whom I have made use', and Nicholas Wynman whom Thevenot thought to be Dutch.[35] His acknowledgement to Digby is a large understatement since his book, like Percey's, is based upon it almost entirely. The preface is indeed original, containing an interesting group of swimming references from classical literature and an allusion (not developed) to the aquatic skills of natives: 'it is certain that the Indians and Negroes surpass all other men in the art of swimming and diving'. The bulk of the book, however, repeats the English swimming practices described by Digby. The introduction, of twelve pages, condenses Digby's first book on the nature, place and time of swimming, while the thirty-nine chapters of the text reproduce the second book in an abridged form with only minor changes. Thevenot evidently read Digby in Latin— there is no sign that he knew of Middleton or Percey—and his work was illustrated with thirty-five plates engraved by Charles Moette. These were also copied from Digby, the artist having simply redrawn the central figures of the original woodcuts in an updated classical style

and without including a background. The work was reprinted three
times during the eighteenth century: in 1769, 1780 and 1782.[36] In
consequence Digby, through Thevenot, was a chief influence on the
history of French swimming down to the French Revolution, though he
never received any credit for being so.

Sadly, the fate of Digby's reputation in England was to be similar. The English translator and printer of Thevenot's work, published in 1699 as *The Art of Swimming* 'illustrated by proper figures
with advice for bathing', evidently had no independent knowledge of
Digby and set down Thevenot's name alone on the title-page.[37] The
English translation was a straightforward version of the French, but
the unknown translator added something of his own in the form of a
'prefatory discourse concerning artificial swimming, or keeping one's
self above water by several small portable engines, in cases of danger'. The interest of this preface, which only runs to eight short
pages, is its proposal that swimming could be improved by applying to
it the scientific principles developed during the second half of the
seventeenth century. The author is concerned to raise questions
rather than to answer them, but he is thoroughly modern in his scientific approach to his topic. First, he says, it is important to
consider the specific gravity of human bodies in water, in order to
obtain 'a perfect knowledge of the forces required for sustentation
and motion'. Second, the swimmer's strokes should be studied according to the principles of mechanics, in order to ascertain 'which of
all those various motions /man/ is capable of making with his arms
and legs are the most serviceable to the different ways of swimming'.
This observation reveals a concept which Digby and Thevenot had not
possessed—that swimming could be improved—and anticipates the
efforts of nineteenth- and twentieth-century experts to bring the
strokes to the utmost degree of efficiency.

Last, the author of 1699 suggests the invention of new artificial aids for swimmers or those who cannot swim. As well as corks
and bladders for floating, which were already in use, 'girdles of
several sorts whereof I hear of one lately invented and very useful'
might be made for support in the water. He goes on to propose in-
ventions which closely resemble the modern inflatable life-belt and

flippers. 'A cylindrical case made of oiled cloth, and kept open on
the inside by iron rings, might be so contrived as to tie round one's
waist, and fastened to keep the water out, and that alone would save
from being drowned.' 'Several little machines might be found very
diverting in swimming to promote expedition: ...contrivances of thin
small planes of wood with valves, or otherwise small hinges, fastened
to the legs or feet might be very serviceable to that end, and perform the part of fishes' fins.' Like its French original, the English translation was later reprinted, in 1764 and 1789, and parts of
it made a final appearance as late as about 1838 in an early Victor-
ian *Art of Swimming and Skating*.[38] In England too, therefore, the
influence of Digby on swimming, though unacknowledged, persisted for
most of the eighteenth century.

CONCLUSION

It cannot be said that swimming was a major activity in Britain between 55 BC and AD 1719. The number of those who could swim must
have been a smaller proportion of the population than today, and vir-
tually excluded the whole female sex. Swimming was mainly confined
to ponds and rivers in the summer months, it was not much done in the
sea, and the techniques in use were slower and less efficient than
modern ones. The study of early swimming is nonetheless worthwhile.
It reveals the physical capabilities and objectives of man in the
past, and helps to fix the limits that he reached. It throws light
on the history of education, through which swimming was advocated and
taught, and on war, health and recreation, the motives which led men
to swim. It contributes to an understanding of the imaginative
writers who treated of swimming, and of their works: Ovid, *Beowulf*,
Marlowe, Shakespeare and *Robinson Crusoe*. The nature even of such
great institutions and movements as medieval feudalism, the Renaissance and the Scientific Revolution become clearer as we observe
their effect upon swimming. Like all athletics, swimming is inseparable from the society in which it is practised; each illuminates the
other. It is also worthy of consideration in its own right, despite

its minority support.   During the centuries we have studied, it did not remain static but showed a capacity for development which anticipated that of modern times.   Specialised instructors, written treatises, competitions, mechanical aids, scientific analysis and artificial pools had all appeared at one time or another by 1700.   If its practitioners fell short of the records established by their present-day counterparts, they did notable feats in armour and under fire, they were hardy and adaptable in natural waters and some of them were versatile acrobats.   Their achievement in relation to their means, perhaps, was not so very inferior to that of their successors today.

References

1. For bibliographical details of Middleton's works, see A.W. Pollard & G.R. Redgrave, *A Short-Title Catalogue of Books Printed in England, 1475-1640*, 2nd ed., vol. ii, London, 1976, pp 129, 153.   *The Famous Historie of Chinon of England* has been edited by W.E. Mead, London, Early English Text Soc., original series, vol. clxv, 1925.

2. *Brasenose College Register, 1509-1909*, 2 vols., Oxford, 1909, i, 59.

3. J. & J.A. Venn, *Alumni Cantabrigienses, Part I: ...to 1751*, iii, 184.

4. Ibid., i, 23.

5. Ibid., iv, 354.

6. Ibid., iii, 184; Longden, *Northamptonshire and Rutland Clergy*, ix, 219.

7. Above, chapter four, note 54.

8. It is mentioned by Sir George Buck in 1615 (below, note 11).

9. James Cleland, *HPΩ-ΠΑΙΔΕΙΑ or The Institvtion of a Yovng Noble Man*, Oxford, 1607, pp 220-1.

10. Henry Peacham, *The Compleat Gentleman*, London, 1622, pp 180-1; ed. V.B. Heltzel, Ithaca, New York, 1962, pp 139-40.

11. Sir George Buck, 'The Third Vniversitie of England', appendix to John Stow, *The Annales or Generall Chronicle of England*, ed.

E. Howes, London, 1615, p 986.

12. Fynes Moryson, *An Itinerary Containing His Ten Yeeres Travell*, 1617, part iii, book i, chapter 2, p 19.

13. Francis Osborn, *Advice to a Son*, Oxford, 1656, p 19.

14. John Locke, *Some Thoughts Concerning Education*, London, 1693, p 7.

15. Robert Burton, *The Anatomy of Melancholy*, London, various editions 1621-52, part ii, section 2, membr. 2.

16. Francis Bacon, *Historia Vitae et Mortis*, London, 1623, pp 253-4, 272, 283, 292-3.

17. Sir Thomas Browne, *Pseudodoxia Epidemica*, London, 1646, book iv, chapter 6, pp 193-5.

18. *The Diary of John Evelyn*, ed. E.S. de Beer, 6 vols., Oxford, 1955, iii, 351, 490, 601.

19. Bacon, *Historia Vitae et Mortis*, p 378.

20. Robert Boyle, *New Experiments Physico-Mechanicall touching the Spring of Air*, London, 1660, pp 375-7.

21. Aphra Behn, *Oroonoko: or, The Royal Slave*, London, 1688, pp 11-12.

22. Daniel Defoe, *The Life and Strange Surprizing Adventures of Robinson Crusoe*, London, 1719, /pp 25, 51, 239-40/.

23. Ibid., /pp 239-40/.

24. Ibid., /p 57/.

25. Ibid., /p 239/.

26. /Sir William Sanderson,/ *Aulicus Coquinarie*, London, 1650, p 145.

27. Above, note 11.

28. William Prynne, *A Divine Tragedie Lately Acted*, 1636, pp 13-14.

29. *The Diary of John Evelyn,* ed. de Beer, iii, 15, 38, 101.

30. Boyle, *Experiments Physico-Mechanicall*, p 376.

31. P. Manning, 'Sport and Pastime in Stuart Oxford', *Surveys and Tokens*, ed. H.E. Salter, Oxford, Oxford Historical Soc., lxxv, 1923, pp 106-7; Anthony Wood, *Life and Times*, ed. A. Clark, vol. iii, ibid., xxvi, 1894, p 306.

32. William Percey, *The Compleat Swimmer*, London, 1658.

33. Ibid., p 49.

34. For an outline of Thevenot's life, see *Biographie Universelle Ancienne et Moderne*, 52 vols., Paris, 1811-28, xlv, 377-83.

35. M. Thevenot, *L'Art de Nager*, Paris, 1696, fol. A6.

36. The most accessible list of editions is in *The National Union Catalog*, vol. 589, London, 1978, pp 540-1.

37. M. Thevenot, *The Art of Swimming*, London, 1699. There is another early usage of the noun 'stroke' on p 16.

38. The editions are listed in *British Museum General Catalogue of Printed Books to 1955*, vol. 237, London, 1964, p 228.

Part Two

A SHORT INTRODUCTION FOR TO LEARN TO SWIM

Translated by Christopher Middleton
from Everard Digby's *De Arte Natandi*

The text which follows is based on the two known copies of Middleton's
translation, by kind permission of the libraries which hold them: the
Beinecke Library of Yale University (N*lb*10 587 Dg) and the Bodleian
Library, Oxford (Malone 646). Neither copy is quite perfect. The
original edition contained 88 pages, divided into eleven signatures
lettered A-L. The Bodleian copy lacks leaves B3, B4 and C1, and leaf
L4 of the Yale copy is damaged. The following edition therefore makes
available a complete text of the work for the first time, modernised
with regard to spelling, punctuation and the use of capital letters.
A few of Middleton's very long sentences have been divided, and three
Latin quotations have been translated in italics. Other editorial additions are placed in square brackets.

The illustrations to Middleton's translation were printed from
the re-used plates of Digby's original work. Middleton's printer,
however, did not match the central panels with their original frames,
but mixed them up and inserted two of the panels upside down. In this
edition, therefore, the illustrations have been reproduced exactly as
they first appeared in Digby's *De Arte Natandi*, with the kind permission of the British Library, London. References have also been added
at the ends of Middleton's main sections to the appropriate book and
chapter of Digby's work.

A Short introduction for

to learne to Swimme.

Gathered out of ⹂*Maſter Digbies Booke*
of the Art of Swimming.
(∵)

And tranſlated into Engliſh for the better in-
ſtruction of thoſe who vnderſtand not
the Latine tongue.

By *Chriſtofer Middleton.*

AT LONDON,
Printed by *Iames Roberts* for Edward
White, and are to be ſold at the little North
doore of Paules Church, at the ſigne
of the Gun. 1595.

To the worshipful and well accomplished gentleman
Master Simon Smith

Sir, the report of your perfection in this faculty hath emboldened
me to presume upon your courtesy, the rather for that as experience
in other things hath taught me how birds of one kind, with mutual
consent, help to support the younger and weaker sort till nature
hath sufficiently enabled them, so doth hope in this thing persuade
me that men of one disposition will as willingly accord in their
commendable exercises tending to profitable ends, as the senseless
fowls of the air naturally agree, mutually to maintain their own
estate. Thus under your thrice worthy protection, as a sufficient
shelter from all the airy buzzards, shroud I myself *until age shall
make me a man,* which if you vouchsafe, it shall embolden me so to
employ my next vacant time as may in some better sort requite your
worshipful favour.

Yours in all dutiful
obedience, *C.M.*

To the Reader

I wrote not this (gentle reader) to derogate from his worth whose
labour first brought this work within the rules of art, and hath
thereby as Virgil for the tillage of the earth, Vegetius for military profession, Hippocrates and Galen for physic, Justinian for
the law, Aristotle, Tully, Euclid, Boethius, Ptolemy for the liberal sciences, Pomponious Mela for cosmography or Mercator for the
globes of the world, though his matter may be of some accounted as
the least, yet for his form deserved commendations with the best.
But, for his learned style exceedeth the capacity of the greater
part of men and the matter itself being so necessary for all, I
have (as I could) gathered his work into a brief compendium for
their better understanding that are ignorant in the Latin tongue.
Thus not to gain the reward of other men's labours, nor to attribute to myself other men's virtues, but to uncurtain that to the
view of all which was only appropriated to a few, have I undergone
this task, which I doubt not will prove as profitable as pleasant.

Farewell.

Of the Art of Swimming

Although from the beginning, amongst all the authors of arts and
sciences, there are few or none which have bestowed any pains in the
explaining or publishing this art of swimming, it being so profitable a thing as it is towards the preserving of man's life when as he
is at any time distressed in the greedy jaws of the swelling sea,
destitute of other help, *although it be praised by no-one, yet is it
praiseworthy in nature.* Although it be by none praised, yet doth
nature itself prefer it sufficiently, especially in man, which above
all fowls of the air, fish of the sea, beasts of the earth or other
creatures whatsoever, excelleth in this faculty as hereafter shall
more at large be expressed. If physic be worthy of commendations in
respect of the nature in purging poisoned humours, driving away con-
tagious diseases and by this means adding longer date unto the life
of man, well then may this art of swimming come within the number of
other sciences, which preserveth the precious life of man amidst the
furious billows of the lawless waters, where neither riches nor
friends, neither birth nor kindred, neither liberal sciences nor
other arts, only itself excepted, can rid him from the danger of
death. Nor is it only to be respected for this great help in extrem-
ity of death, but it is also a thing necessary for every man to use,
even in the pleasantest and securest time of his life, especially as
the fittest thing to purge the skin from all external pollutions or
uncleanness whatsoever, as sweat and such like, as also it helpeth to
temperate the extreme heat of the body in the burning time of the
year. And if we respect thoroughly the nature of this art, we may
easily perceive and see that it doth not much differ from the rest of
the liberal sciences *proceeding from a free mind.* (I. 1-4)

Whether all things swim by nature, or no

Nature, our provident mother, hath carefully provided for every several creature several means for their preservation in their several
kinds. As unto those creatures which have their living in the inmost
bowels of the earth or other such places far remote from the danger

of water, to those hath she not imparted this knowledge for that is
a thing to them altogether impertinent. But to other her creatures,
either those whose continual abode is in the deeps as fishes, fowls
and some beasts that live in the water, or to other which in the actions of their lives do any ways tend towards the waters, on them for
their better preservation hath she bestowed this great gift, yet not
to every creature alike, but what element doth most abound in the
composition of their bodies, according to the quality thereof is
their kind of swimming. As for example a toad hath a broader body
than a frog and to man's judgment more fit to swim. And yet because
her complexion is more earthly and therefore heavier by nature and
feedeth upon the solid poison of the earth, either presently after
she cometh into the water sinketh right down, or if she do remain any
time upon the superficies of the water, it is with great labour.
Whereas a frog, feeding on the airy dew that lieth upon the grass,
pleasantly playeth upon the water, lively representing the true swimming of a man.

The like reasons is of the fowls of the air, as the swallows
that feed upon the slender buzzing flies of the air, they nimblier
fly to and fro and lightlier drink on the top of the water than other
fowls, that either feed on the worms of the earth or the fishes of
the sea. And even as the lifeless trunks, which in their constitution have a greater temperature of air or fire than of water or earth,
are of their own accord carried above the water as wood and such-like,
and on the contrary heavy constitutions of water or earth as lead,
iron, stone and such directly settle down to the bottom, so is it
with all creatures that have life. As the lion, the beast of the sun
and king of the forest, because he is of a sanguine complexion, a hot
constitution, nimble of his joints and of a noble courage, swims
lightly and strongly, and so of the dog and other creatures whose
constitution is a lower degree of heat. But some kinds of fowls, although they be of a good constitution of body, yet for some impedi-
ment in their form are hindered and do not swim so well as other
whose bodies are more gross. As the cock, which is the bird of the
sun, for that he wanteth (as we call them) the webs of his feet, swimmeth not so easily as a duck which is more melancholy and heavy by

nature according to the disposition of Saturn. (I. 5-6)

Man swimmeth by nature

The fishes in the sea, whose continual life is spent in the water, in
them doth no man deny swimming to be the only gift which nature hath
bestowed upon them. And shall we think it then artificial in a man,
which in it doth by many degrees excel them—as diving down to the
bottoms of the deepest waters and fetching from thence whatsoever is
there sunk down, transporting things to and fro at his pleasure, sitting, tumbling, leaping, walking—and at his ease performeth many
fine feats in the water which far exceeds the natural gifts bestowed
on fishes? Nay, so fit is the constitution of man's body that whoso
doth but with himself thoroughly consider of it cannot but accord
with me in this, that a man of all creatures under the circumference
of heaven naturally excelleth in swimming.

As for example, a shaft shot in the water, when it riseth again
hangeth perpendicularly downward with the head, and the upper parts
and feathers swim above the water. Even so is it with a man, who
although the lower parts of his body be earthly and heavy, yet above
is the life of lives, the vital spirits, the external and internal
senses. To be short, the life spirits of every man exceedeth the
lives of all beasts, for that they /the beasts/ only retain the veg-
etable and sensual powers, the one whereby they grow and increase and
the other whereby they hear, feel, see, smell and taste. But in man
is all these, whose least part exceedeth the greatest quantity of the
other in the highest degree: a reasonable soul. So that he hath not
only in great measure the other helps which nature hath provided for
this purpose, but he hath wisdom by art to perfect that in himself
which by nature is left imperfect. And having plain rules of art how
by motion to keep up the heavy parts of his body, which by reason of
their heaviness are naturally carried down, it cannot otherwise be
but that swimming must naturally come to a man, and in swimming he
must excel all creatures whatsoever.

But, for some will object that if swimming were so natural a
thing to a man then should not so many perish in the water, to these

in a word I thus answer: that men who have not had some practice in
it afore, when by any sinister occasion they fall into the water, the
discreet use of their senses is taken away by a sudden fear. And so
unorderly labouring in the water, they by the indirect moving of
their bodies pull down themselves under the water and so are drowned,
which to avoid I leave it to every several man's consideration how
necessary a thing this art of swimming is. (I. 7-8)

Of the place and time to swim

Of all the circumstances which the author of this our art hath in his
first book learnedly set down, as necessary antecedents before he
enter into the practice itself, I hold these two sufficient for the
unlearned sort to know: time and place, and leave the rest to their
wise considerations which are able thoroughly to understand the Latin
tongue. The time which the temperature of this our climate affords
as good to swim in, is comprehended in four months: May, June, July
and August, for that in these months the sun drawing nearer unto our
zenith, his beams falling more directly down upon the superficies of
this earth make a greater reflection, and thence cometh a more vehement heat which doth temperate the water and make wholesome the air.
The wind and weather ought also in these months to be regarded, especially of those whose weak constitution is not so able to endure the
cold as others of a stronger composition of body. The winds that are
most unwholesome and dangerous to swim in is the east and north, for
that blowing from cold and dry places they bring divers and sundry
discommodities. The weather that is to be eschewed is rain, for
these considerations: the drops do trouble the superficies of the
water, hurteth the body, disturbeth the eyes and lastly, draining
from the banks into the river, bringeth also with it whatsoever dung,
straw, leaves and what filth or unwholesome things else, do lie near
adjoining unto the place. (I. 9-14)

In the place is two things especially to be respected. First,
that the banks be not overgrown with rank thick grass where oft-times
do lie and lurk many stinging serpents and poisoned toads; not full
of thorns, briars, stubs or thistles which may offend the bare feet,

but that the grass be short, thin and green, the bank beset with
shady trees which may be a shelter from the wind and a shadow from
the parching heat of the sun. Next, that the water itself be clear,
not troubled with any kind of slimy filth which is very infectious
to the skin; that the breadth, depth and length thereof be sufficiently known; that it be not muddy at the bottom, lest by much treading, the filth rising up from the bottom thicken the water, and so
make it unfit for that purpose. Also that there be not in the bottom
of the river any old stakes or sharp stones, which may greatly en-
danger the swimmer, but that it be a clear running water not a standing corrupted pool, the bottom fair sand, where from the banks may
easily be perceived whatsoever doth lie in the deepest place of the
river.

    Which time and place, according to these rules and directions
when he hath fitly selected, let him associate himself with someone
that is taller and stronger than himself which may both comfort him
and help to sustain him, for that at the first entrance the chillness
of the water will greatly discomfort him, as also he may thereby be
better directed where the water is deep and where it is shallow. But
if so be that he for any extraordinary occasion or other reason whatsoever rather delight to be alone, then thus. Let him take a long
rod like unto an angle, and upon the end thereof hang in a long small
cord a plummet of lead, wherewith he may standing upon the bank sound
every place of the water. And if he cannot reach the further side
with his pole, boldly venturing so far into the water as by this direction he hath experienced, he may reach further and further until he
hath tried it all. Which, if he find correspondent in every point to
the rules before rehearsed, and that there be not any sudden or plumb
falling down into any great holes which exceed his own height, nor
any whirlpools as we call them, or kind of swift or violent streams
that may forcely carry him away, let him there practise according to
these rules following, and venture not into any other unknown place
until he be a perfect practitioner in this art. Thus much for the
time and place. (I. 15-16)

To enter the water

For the manner of his going into the river, it must not be sweating,
a thing whereunto in the heat of the summer men are greatly subject,
for that coming into the cold water it maketh a sudden change in body
which is very dangerous. But rather, by walking easily in some cool
shade or some such other moderate means, let him before he enter into
the water bring his body into a reasonable temperature of heat and
cold. And then not as some, which are more bold than wise, rudely
leap into the water with their feet downward, as this picture next
following showeth:

But let him easily enter until he be covered up to the waist in water,
as thus: (II. 1)

Peri·

But when he can perfectly swim and boldly turn himself every way in
the water, then were it better to leap than to go in: laying his
hands on his neck and forcibly running to /the/ bank, where declin-
ing his head downwards and turning round over with his heels, he may
light into the water upon his back, as in this example: (II. 1)

Or, when he cometh at the side, fall upon his right or left side
after this fashion: (II. 1)

Or else, leaping from the bank and casting forth his legs (but yet keeping of them close together), he may light upon his hips and the hinder parts of his legs, as you see in this picture: (II. 1)

The first degree of swimming

These directions are sufficient either for his entrance which is yet
to learn, or for his which is already expert in this faculty. Now he
that is learning to swim, as we said afore, having waded in up to the
waist or somewhat higher, laying himself easily along upon the water
with his belly downward, and striving as much as he can to hold up
his head, and draw/ing/ in his arms close to his breast, holding his
hands broadways together under his chin with the palms down; let him
pull his feet from the bottom and withal put forth his hands as far
as he can and draw them in again as afore, and likewise his feet.
Which double motion of hands and feet serve to this use: the one
thrusteth him forward and the other keepeth up his body. And because
it is a toil, something to learn how to strike right thus with his
hands and feet as afore, let him either get someone to accompany him
that may by holding his hand under his chin keep him from sinking, or
else take two bladders, blow them full of wind and fasten them so
together that he may have them to lie under his armholes, which will
easily bear him up. And thus may he do till he hath perfectly
learned to swim on his belly, as the picture following showeth:
(II. 2)

To *⎾turn⏌* on the back

But, for that with long swimming on his belly he will be wearied,
nature that provident nurse, which carefully provideth for every
creature things fitting their kind, hath as in all things so in this
thing made man excel everything. For him hath she taught in this to
ease his weary arms by lying in the water upon his back, which we
call 'swimming upon the back'——a gift which she hath denied even to
the watery inhabitants of the sea. No fish, no fowl, nor other
creature whatsoever that hath any living or being, either in the
depth of the sea or superficies of the water, swimmeth upon his back,
man only excepted. And therefore, when he hath perfectly learned to
swim to and fro on his belly as he listeth, let him learn thus to
turn upon his back by thrusting out his right hand as far as he can
before him, and withal turn over his left side, and still keep out
his right hand until he be turned upon his back, for that it doth in
turning so support him from sinking, as in this example following:
(II. 3)

/To swim on the back/

And when he is thus laid upon his back, he must lie very straight,
not bending or bowing with his body any way, save only his legs
which he must easily pull out and in, as when he was on his belly,
to put him forwards in the water, as thus: (II. 4)

To turn in the water like a roach

There is another kind of turning when a man is swimming upon his belly with his head one way: suddenly to turn himself, still being upon his belly, and bring about his head and all his body the other way. And for that it is to be done quickly (as oft times you may see the fishes within the water, when in the pleasant heat of summer they wantonly frisk to and fro), it is commonly called 'the roach turn', and that is done thus. If he will turn towards the right hand, he must suddenly put the water from him with his left hand, and pull that water behind towards him with his right hand, turning back his head and his body as you see in this next figure: (II. 5)

To turn 'the bell turn' in the water

There is also a turning which is called 'the bell turn', as when one
swimming on his belly shall suddenly pull in his feet, and instead
of striking with them as is aforesaid, he shall, heaving backward
with his foreparts, strike forward with his feet, which motion will
turn him upon his back. And because he may at his pleasure turn so
upon his back and belly as he will, it is called 'the bell turn',
resembling also a bell when it is ringing, as for example: (II. 6)

To tumble in the water

There is also a kind of tumbling in the water, as a man would roll
and tumble in the grass, and that is done thus. Swimming on his
belly or back, which way he meaneth to roll himself—as towards the
right hand or the left, he must thrust that hand broad-ways down
into the water with the palm downward, and he must carry the other
/hand/ close beside him as ready to use on the other side. And with
the uppermost leg still as he turneth, strike the superficies of the
water so that the motion with the hand helpeth to turn over the body.
And the striking with the feet keepeth better up the hindmost parts,
which are most heavy of themselves, as in this picture following:
(II. 7)

To strike the superficies of the water

To strike the superficies of the water with four parts of the body
at twice is thus done: by lying upon your back and something de-
clining your body towards the left side, which hand must be in the
water, labouring to and fro like the fin of a fish, to keep him
from sinking. And so he may lift his right hand and right leg out
of the water and beat them down again, and so of the left side, as
the picture following showeth: (II. 16)

To swim with hands and feet upward

To swim with hands and feet upward is nothing else but the swimming
upon the back as we taught before, saving that he useth his hands
as a boat doth her oars, casting them out on both sides and drawing
them in again, which maketh his motion swifter, as in this example:
(II. 17)

To swim backward

That is when one, lying upon his back with his body stretched forth,
and holding up his breast as much as he can that his back may lie
hollow, which will keep him from sinking, and lifting easily one
foot after another above the water, and so drawing them forcibly
towards him under the water, they will pull his body backward, as
in this example is showed: (II. 18)

To roll upon one's back

This is done only by lying straight upon his back and pressing down the water with his hands, so may he roll from side to side like a ship at sea, as thus: (II. 19)

To make a circle in the water with his feet

This is done as we said afore, by lying straight upon his back without bending any part of his body. And if he will turn from the
right hand, then must he lie somewhat over upon his left side, and
first of all pull his right leg out of the water and afterwards
his left as fast as he can, and strike with them toward the left
hand, one after another, and about one foot, one before another,
which will turn his body round and make his head lie in the midst,
like the centre of a circle, as thus: (II. 8)

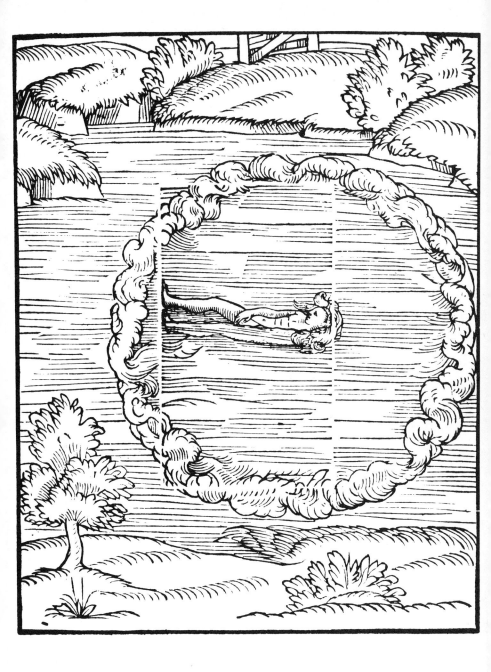

To stand upright and turn about in the water

He must by stirring of his feet up and down in the water keep up his
body, and keeping his hands underneath the water, pull the water towards him that way which he would turn, and so also incline the
motion of his feet, as thus: (II. 9)

To swim with his hands together

This must be done in all respects as is said afore for the first
kind of swimming upon the belly, saving the motion of the hands
which must be joined with their palms together, the thumbs standing right upward, which he must pull into his breast and thrust
them forth again without parting of them, as for example: (II. 10)

To swim upon his side

This kind of swimming, though it be more laborious, yet is it
swifter than any of the rest, for that lying upon one side, striking with your feet as when you swim on your belly, but that the
pulling in and thrusting out of his hand, which then did only keep
him up, do now help to put him forward. For only the lower hand
supporteth his body, and the upper hand roweth like an oar, as in
this example: (II. 11)

To swim upon his belly with his hands still

This is only to lay his hands behind him and strain himself to bear
up his head somewhat higher, and strike somewhat lower with his feet,
as in the picture following is showed: (II. 12)

To swim with one hand and one foot upon his belly

He must take his right foot backwards in his left hand, and strike
with his right hand and left foot; which, for that one is upon the
one side and the other on the other, they will easily bear him up,
as thus:

The use of these two last kinds of swimming is to ease his
hands that is subject to the cramp or any other infirmity. (II. 13)

To swim like a dog

Into this kind of swimming many do at the first fall, before they
perfectly learn the right stroke. And there is this difference
betwixt them, that whereas in the right kind ⎾of stroke⏌ he
stretcheth out his hands and his feet, in this he rudely beateth
the water with his hands and feet, first lifting his right hand
out of the water and then his right foot, and forcibly striking
them into the water again, as in this example following: (II. 14)

To beat the water

This is done swimming upon his back and lying straight out with his
body, the palms of his hands being downward, and moving up and down
in the water to keep him up. So may he lift out either one or other
of his legs, and beat with it upon the superficies of the water at
his pleasure, as thus: (II. 15)

To play above the water with one foot

This is all one with the next precedent, saving that instead of
striking his leg right down into the water, he must, turning it
about three or four times, only but touch the very superficies
of the water with his toe, as in this example: (II. 20)

To show his toes above the water

This is also done by lying straight upon his back, stretching out
his feet together at length, and moving with his hands in the water
as in the former example, and so lifting up his feet till he hath
brought all his toes above the water, as thus: (II. 21)

To hang by the chin in the water

When he is swimming upon his back, let his feet sink easily down
towards the bottom, and withal let him strive as much as in him lies
to bend in his back, bowing backwards his head, until his face be
the uppermost part of his body. And then draw his feet somewhat up-
wards, his hands holden behind his back and his body bending also
that ways like unto a bow, so that the water, working up and down in
the concavity of his back, will so easily hold up his body that he
shall not need to stir either with hand or foot, as thus: (II. 22)

To tread the water

This is only standing bolt up as it were in the water, and pulling
up your feet and thrusting them down again, after the same manner
as he doth swimming upon his belly, which have the same force to
keep him that way which they have to thrust him forwards the other
way, as you may see in this picture next following: (II. 23)

To swim with one hand and one foot upon his back

This is the same upon the back which the other was upon the belly:
to lie upon your back, and behind you take your left leg in your
right hand, and forcibly move your other leg as when you swim upon
your back, thus: (II. 24)

To swim with his hands and feet bound

This kind of swimming is easiliest done by lying very straight upon his back, drawing in his legs and thrusting them forth again, after this manner: (II. 25)

To slide forwards upon his belly in the water

This must be thus done. He must keep his hands together with their
palms downwards, by which he must draw the water towards him; and
his feet also and legs kept close together, he must easily thrust
out and keep in as well as he can, keeping them together in this
wise:

This is best to be used in those rivers where are many high
weeds, for that swimming upon his belly thus, he shall safelier
slide over them. (II. 26)

To sit in the water

He that will exercise this kind of swimming must be such a one as is
not troubled with the cramp, for that the forcible bending backward
with his body is otherwise very dangerous, which must be thus done.
Lying upon his back, he must draw in his feet towards his hips, and
use some motion with his hands under the water to sustain him till
he hath gotten his legs in his hands, thus:

And then, using some small motion to put him forwards, keeping
only his breast and head above the water, the stream will easily
keep him up by reason of the concavity in the back. (II. 27)

To pare his toes in the water

Swimming upon his back, let him draw up his left foot and lay it over his right knee, still keeping his body very straight, and then having a knife ready in his right hand, he may easily keep up his leg until he hath pared one of his toes, as thus: (II. 28)

To show four parts of his body above the water at once

He must lie straight upon his back and lay one leg over the other
knee, so that the uppermost knee may easily be seen above the water.
Then he must, setting his hands on his breast, hold up his elbows
above the water, and so he shall at once show his head, his elbows
and one knee, as thus: (II. 29)

To swim with one leg right up

That must, as the rest, be done by lying straight upon his back and
lifting one leg as high above the water as he can, and striking under
the water with his other leg to drive him forwards, his hand easily
moving by his side the better to keep him up, as in this example:
(II. 30)

To carry anything dry over the water in his hands

This is only done by swimming upon his back and straining himself to
lie straight with his body, so that he hold his arms straight up,
which will else force him to bend his body and so he shall sink.　And
holding his arms upward as afore, he may easily carry or recarry any
thing over the water without wetting, as for example: (II. 31)

To stroke his leg as if he were pulling on a boot

This is nothing else but lying straight upon his back, as are all
the other extraordinary feats, and suddenly lifting one leg above
the water, stroke with both his hands in this manner: (II. 32)

To caper with both his legs at once above the water

Lying upon his back, straight as afore, his hands with their palms
downwards pressing the water the better to keep him up, he must cast
both his legs out of the water at once, and caper with them upward
as men use to do downward in dancing, as thus: (II. 33)

To dive underneath the water

He must, if he be in a place where he may stand upon the ground,
with as much force as he can, leap up, and bending his head towards his breast fall forwards down into the water, as thus: (II. 34)

⎣To descend beneath the water⎦

His hands must he hold before his head with their backs together,
that they may be ready to pull him as it were forcing him down
under the water, and he must, pulling them out and in, now use
them to help him down which were afore a means to hold him up.
His feet also must strike upward, moving them after the same
manner as he doth swimming above the water upon his belly, after
this example: (II. 35)

To swim under the water

When he hath thus buried himself in the water, he must thrust his
hands forth before his head and, as it were, draw the waters which
are before and beat them behind him, /and/ strike with his feet as
swimming upon his belly, but somewhat upward that they may the
easilier keep him down, as in this example: (II. 36)

To rise from the bottom

That is done by the speedy turning upward of his body and with one
hand, the palm being downwards, press down the water beneath him,
and with the other hand draw down the water which is above him, and
then striking downwards with his feet it will easily bring him up,
as thus: (II. 37)

To seek any thing that is lost in the water

He must swim under the water as afore but as near the bottom as he
can, so that he touch it not lest he raise any mud to thicken the
water, his eyes open that he may see where it lieth. And if so be
that he have any occasion to turn himself, or to seek round about
as thinking himself near the thing he seeketh, if he will turn towards the left hand, he must with his right hand pull towards him
the water which is on his left side, which will easily turn him
about, as this picture next following showeth by example:

But thus much to him which learneth to dive: let him never
swim further than he can see the bottom, for it is either very deep
or else he is under some bank, or in some such danger. (II. 38)

To swim like a dolphin

This is nothing else but in diving to lift his head above the water,
and when he hath breathed, presently dive down again, as afore:
(II. 39)

FINIS

BIBLIOGRAPHY

EARLY SWIMMING TREATISES

Digby, Everard. *De Arte Natandi*, London, 1587.

Digby, Everard. *A Short Introduction for to Learne to Swimme*, trans-translated by Middleton, Christopher, London, 1595.

Percey, William. *The Compleat Swimmer: or, the Art of Swimming*, London, 1658.

Thevenot, Melchisedech. *L'Art de Nager*, Paris, 1696.

Thevenot, Melchisedech. *The Art of Swimming*, London, 1699.

Wynman, Nicolaus. *Colymbetes, sive de arte natandi dialogus*, Augsburg, 1538.

Wynman, Nicolaus. *Nicol. Wynmanni Colymbetes... das erste Schwimmbuch der Welt*, ed. Wassmannsdorf, K., Heidelberg, 1889.

MODERN WORKS

Brailsford, D. *Sport and Society: Elizabeth to Anne*, London, 1969.

McIntosh, P.C. *Landmarks in the History of Physical Education*, 3rd edition, London, 1981.

Mehl, E. 'Schwimmen', in *Paulys Real-Encyclopädie der Classischen Altertumswissenschaft*, ed. Wissova, G., & Kroll, W., supplement, vol. v, Stuttgart, 1931.

Thomas, Ralph. *Swimming, with lists of books published in English, German, French and other European Languages*, 2nd edition, London, 1904.

Vale, Marcia. *The Gentleman's Recreations: Accomplishments and Pastimes of the English Gentleman, 1580-1630*, Ipswich, 1977.

West, M. 'Spenser, Everard Digby and the Renaissance Art of Swimming', *Renaissance Quarterly*, vol. xxvi, 1973, pp 11-22.

Zeigler, E.F. *A History of Sport and Physical Education to 1900 (Selected Topics)*, Champagne, Illinois, 1973.

INDEX

Agricola, 2

Ajax Oileus, legend of, 30-1, 62

Alexander the Great, 29-30

Alexander Severus, Emperor, 53

Allott, Robert, 93

Alphonsi, Peter, 28-9

Alvey, Henry, 75-6

Anglesey, 2

Anglo-Saxon swimming, 9-13

Apollonius of Tyre, 13, 62

Ascham Roger, 52

Augustus, Emperor, 4, 28

Bacon, Sir Francis, 98-9

Barbour, John, 36

Bartholomaeus Anglicus, 36

Batavi, 7, 8-9, 10

Bath, Som., 3, 37-8, 103

Behn, Aphra, 101

Benoit of Ste. Maure, 30

Beowulf, 10-12

Berry, duke of, *Tres Riches
      Heures* of, 38-40

Bible and swimming, 22-4, 47-9

Boyle, Hon. Robert, 100, 103

Breca, 11-12

Browne, Sir Thomas, 99

Buck, Sir George, 97, 102

Burton, Robert, 98-9

Buxton, Derbys., 3

Caesar, Julius, 1, 2, 8, 10, 59-
      60, 70, 97

Caligula - see Gaius

Calvin, John, 48-9

Cambridge, 55, 56, 64-5, 72-9, 82,
      88, 93

Cardano, Girolamo, 98

Castiglione, Baldassare, 52

Cato, Marcus Portius, 4

Caxton, William, 29, 31

Cessoles, Jacques de, 25, 28

Chaloner, Sir Thomas, 62

Charles II, 99

Chretien de Troyes, 32

Christine de Pisan, 28

Church and swimming, 22-6, 47-9,
      102-3

Cicero, 4

Cleland, James, 96-7

Cornelius a Lapide, 23-4, 47-8

Coverdale, Miles, 23-4

Culhwch and Olwen, 13

Dares of Phrygia, 30

Defoe, Daniel, 101-2

Dictys Cretensis, 30

Digby, Everard, mentioned, 54, 55,
      56, 64, 94, 116
   origins of, 71-2
   at Cambridge, 72-9
   writings of, 73-4, 79-81
   De Arte Natandi of, 74, 81-8,
      94-5, 104-7
   expulsion from Cambridge, 75-9
   final years, 79-81

diving, 11, 13, 15-16, 16-17, 49-
        50, 100, 103, 105, 196-207
Domitian, Emperor, 5
Drake, Sir Francis, 49
Drayton, Michael, 93

Edward II, 34-5
Egil's Saga, 15-16
Elegabalus, Emperor, 5
Elyot, Sir Thomas, 52-3, 96-7
Evelyn, John, 99-100, 103
Eystein, King, 17

FitzStephen, William, 35

Gaius, Emperor, 4
Garzoni, Tommaso, 70, 97
Germani, 10
Gerrard, 63
Giles of Rome, 25, 28
Gregory the Great, 24-5
Grettir's Saga, 15-16
Griffyn, Master, 36
Guarino da Verona, 50
Guido delle Colonne, 30
Guylforde, Sir Richard, 49

Hadrian, Emperor, 7, 8-9
Hervey, 63
Haymo of Halberstadt, 41
Heimskringla, 15, 17
Henry Stuart, Prince of Wales,
        102
Herbert, Edward, Lord, 63-4
Hero - see Leander
Herve of Bourg-Dieu, 41

Hood, Robin, 37, 44
Horace, 4, 19, 28, 51
Horman, William, 51

Jerome, Saint, 23, 47
John of Salisbury, 25, 28

Kali-Rognvald, 15-16
knights, medieval, 25, 26-35

Langland, William, 25, 35-6
Laxdale Saga, 15, 16-17
Leander, 6, 57-8, 104
Lefevre, Raoul, 31
Livy, 53
Locke, John, 98
London, 35-6, 63, 64, 97, 102
Lusitanians, 7
Luttrell, Sir John, 63
Lydgate, John, 25, 31

Mabinogion, The, 13-14
Magnus, Saint, 14, 16
Malory, Sir Thomas, 32-3, 35
'Mandeville, Sir John', 50
Marlowe, Christopher, 56-8
Mejia, Pedro, 70, 97
Middleton, Christopher, mentioned,
        63, 64, 87
    career of, 92-4
    writings of, 92
    Short Introduction of, 94-6,
        111-207
miracles, 24-5
More, Sir Thomas, 50-1
Moryson, Fynes, 97

Mulcaster, Richard, 52, 53-4, 55

Njal's Saga, 15
Normans and swimming, 22-33

Olaf Haraldsson, King, 14
Olaf Tryggvason, King, 14, 16, 17
Orkneyinga Saga, 15
Orosius, 12-13
Osborn, Francis, 98
Ovid, 3, 4, 6, 57-8
Oxford, 64, 103

Pakington, Sir John, 63
Paris, Matthew, 50
Peacham, Henry, 63, 96-7
Percey, William, 103-5
Petronilla of Ardres, 37
Plautus, 4, 51
Pliny the Younger, 5
Plutarch, 1, 2, 53
Prynne, William, 102-3

Raleigh, Sir Walter, 50
Robert of Reading, 25, 34-5
Roman swimming, 1-9, 27, 50-1
Rothe, Johannes, 28-9

sagas, 14-18
Sanderson, Sir William, 102
Scaeva, Cassius, 18, 70
Scandinavia - see Vikings
Scotland, 16, 34, 36
Seneca the Younger, 5
Sertorius, 7-8
Shakespeare, William, 58-62

Sidney, Sir Philip, 63
Sigurd Jerusalem-Farer, King,
     14, 17-18
Smith, Simon, 63, 92, 115
Snorri Sturluson, 15
Spenser, Edmund, 54-6, 63
Steen, Cornelius van den - see
     Cornelius a Lapide
Suebi, 10
Suetonius, 1, 4, 5, 8, 28, 53
swimming, attitudes to
     erotic and romantic, 5-6, 37,
          57-8
     favourable, 1-2, 4-7, 12-14,
          15, 18, 25-6, 27-8, 31, 35,
          46-9, 50, 52-4, 56-8, 61,
          81-3, 96-8, 99, 100-2, 103-7
     religious, 22-6, 47-9, 102-3
     scientific, 83, 98-100, 106-7
     unfavourable, 23-5, 31-3, 35,
          37, 50, 58-65, 98, 102-3
swimming, by whom done,
     aristocracy, 1, 4-5, 11-15, 17,
          26-35, 52-3, 55-6, 62-5, 88,
          97, 102-3
     children and youths, 4-6, 11,
          51, 54, 60, 63-5, 82, 98,
          102-3
     females, 4, 10, 15, 37-8, 57,
          104
     males, passim (most references)
     natives (non-Europeans), 49-51,
          100-2, 105
     non-aristocracy,
          2, 4, 15, 35-7, 64-5,
          102-3

swimming, how done,
   accidents during, 6, 34, 35-6,
       59-61, 64-5, 82, 97-8,
       102-3
   armour, wearing, 8-9, 11-12,
       32-3, 51, 55-6, 70
   artificial aids, use of, 4, 7,
       16, 36, 51, 60, 87, 106-7
   clothes, wearing, 16, 37-8,
       59, 102
   competitive, 5, 11-12, 16-17,
       36, 59-60, 63, 87-8
   distances covered, 1, 7, 11,
       16, 63, 102
   horses, with, 2, 7, 9, 32-3,
       43, 52, 55-6, 64, 66-7
   nude, 6, 16, 17, 31, 35-8, 40,
       8, 63, 85, 102, 103
   pictures of, 38-40, 43, 63,
       84-5, 95, 105-6
   strokes, kinds of, 38-40, 63,
       69-70, 84-8, 95
   terminology used for, 87, 95-
       6, 104-5, 110
swimming, how learnt,
   learning and teaching in prac-
       tise, 5, 7, 27, 40, 51, 54,
       63-4, 69, 84, 102, 104
   treatises on, 3-4, 69-71, 74,
       81-8, 94-5, 103-7
swimming, motives for,
   health, 4-5, 10, 53-4, 82-3,
       98-9, 101, 102-4
   life-saving of other people,
       87, 97-8
   military, 1, 2, 6-9, 11,

swimming, motives for - continued
   military - continued, 26-33,
       51, 52, 63, 96-7
   practical and utilitarian, 15-
       16, 35, 64, 82-3, 97-8, 104
   recreation, 4-5, 16-18, 34-5,
       37, 83, 98, 103-4
swimming, where done,
   artificial pools, 3, 5, 37, 98
   lakes and ponds, 11, 15-16,
       36-8, 54-5, 64, 70, 84, 103
   rivers, 2-6, 7-10, 13, 16-18,
       23, 25, 27, 32, 34-40, 54-5,
       59, 63-4, 70, 84, 95, 98,
       102-3
   sea, 1, 2, 6, 7, 11, 14, 15-16,
       23-5, 30-1, 49-50, 54, 56-8,
       60-1, 62-3, 70, 97, 102

Tacitus, 2, 70
Thames, River, 35-6, 63, 102-3
Thevenot, Melchisedech, 70, 105-6
Thomas Becket, Saint, 25
Tiber, River, 3-5, 7, 59
Troy literature, medieval, 30-1

Valturio, Roberto, 66
Vatable, François, 48
Vegetius Renatus, Flavius, 7,
       26-8, 52, 56, 97
Viking and Norse swimming, 11-12,
       14-18
Virgil, 5-6, 57
Vulgate - see Bible

Wales and Welsh swimming, 2, 13-14,

Wales - continued, 36   Whitaker, William, 75-9
water-jousting, 35   Whitgift, John, 64, 76-9
Weever, John, 93   Wroxeter, Salop, 3
Well, Yorks., 3   Wynman, Nicholas, 69-71, 105